I0816213

MURDER ON THE MISSISSIPPI

ALSO BY SALADIN AMBAR

Malcolm X at Oxford Union:
Racial Politics in a Global Era

American Cicero:
Mario Cuomo and the Defense
of American Liberalism

Stars and Shadows:
The Politics of Interracial Friendship
from Jefferson to Obama

MURDER ON THE MISSISSIPPI

The Shocking Crimes That Shaped Abraham Lincoln

SALADIN AMBAR

DIVERSION BOOKS

Diversion Books
A division of Diversion Publishing Corp.
www.diversionbooks.com

For more information, email info@diversionbooks.com

First Diversion Books Edition: October 2025
Hardcover ISBN: 979-8-89515-021-4
e-ISBN: 979-8-89515-020-7

Design by Neuwirth & Associates, Inc.
Cover design by Jonathan Sainsbury / 6x9 Design

Printed in the United States of America
1 3 5 7 9 10 8 6 4 2

→ ←

This book is dedicated to the memory of Francis McIntosh and all those who have faced down the mob, in any form and in every generation. Your stories matter, and your courage in the darkest of hours remains an inspiration. As the great antifascist Antonio Gramsci remarked in his own dark time, "The old world is dying, and the new world struggles to be born: Now is the time of monsters." Our debt to you is to continue opposing the monsters arrayed against us as best we can, in our time. May your memories be a blessing.

CONTENTS

PROLOGUE

"Horrible Tragedy! Mulatto Man Burned Alive in St. Louis!"

His heart was pounding as he ran from the dock, his bright red jacket flapping in the early evening breeze. A gambler down in New Orleans had given it to him and he was anxious to show it off. There was just enough daylight left in the late April sky to impress the people of St. Louis with his stylish prize before he met the woman he was there to see—a woman he had recently grown quite fond of. As soon as the *Flora* docked, his work as steward behind him, he bounded down the gangway filled with expectation. But now, as the sky darkened, the young Black man found himself running for his life, the blood in his calves pumping hard, with a screaming constable trailing at his heels. Despite the swarm of confusion in his head, he could make out the wild eyes of white men on the street gazing upon him. The beautiful spring Thursday he had planned had taken a fearsome turn. And the woman he was to meet—a chambermaid from another boat he had been courting—would never see him alive again. Within minutes of disembarking, the sun was going down on twenty-six-year-old Francis McIntosh of Pittsburgh. He had just cut a white sheriff's throat with a knife, dropping the man dead in a pool of his own blood, and the world would care little to hear how or why.

When the constable called out to onlookers for help during the chase, McIntosh was finally cornered and brought to the ground. He was taken to the city jail in St. Louis and put in a cell to await his fate. But McIntosh already suspected what that fate was, though he scarcely could have known how grim it would be. That is because, before he was pursued that night by what passed for St. Louis's police at the time, he had witnessed another man in flight from the same officer. That man fled directly in front of McIntosh moments after he had gotten off the *Flora*. Two officers called out to him to grab the suspect—but McIntosh, his mind on getting to his date, ignored them. Unsatisfied with failing to apprehend their man, the officers grabbed McIntosh instead, arresting him on the spot for failing to comply.

By some accounts, as the officers walked him to jail, McIntosh was told that he was as good as dead—or bound to prison for life—for this indiscretion. That is when McIntosh—a free Black man in a slave state—realized the enormity of the stakes confronting him. And that is when, attempting to free himself, he lunged at one officer with his knife and missed. But as the other officer approached, McIntosh's blade found its target, and the man, a deputy sheriff named George Hammond, clutched at the gaping wound in his throat, then took some twenty paces before collapsing dead on the street. Thus began the chase that led to McIntosh's capture and detention in St. Louis's jail on the night of April 28, 1836.

In a different country, in a different time, that might have been the end of it. McIntosh would have had the right to face a jury of his peers. He would have had a right to counsel and to tell his side of the story. And the surviving officer, William Mull, would have been able to confront him in a court of law. Instead, McIntosh was confined to his cell and heard the growing cries of a mob that surrounded him. Their screams grew louder as they moved closer, ultimately overwhelming the guard and breaking into the jail. The word had spread quickly in town that a mulatto—a "yellow fellow" as McIntosh was later described in the press—had taken the life of a white man, and before long, he was enveloped by a multitude of St. Louisans in a state of frenzy, their high-pitched wailings and lamentations fueling a collective bloodlust. Indecipherable chants rose from the mob as they marched a terrified McIntosh westward, finally stopping in front of an old locust tree on the edge of town, somewhere around Seventh and Chestnut Streets. Finally, with a torrent of people closing tightly around him, McIntosh could make out the chants. "Burn him! Burn him!" they screamed, as he was chained to the tree.

Hundreds looked on as members of a local fire company placed kindling around McIntosh's feet. Then, as the fire was lit and the smoke went up, the jeers rose to a fevered pitch. Within minutes, as the flames tore through his lower body, his chest heaving in agony, McIntosh somehow summoned the strength to call out to the crowd, begging to be shot. He received no such mercy, as the mob—one that was thought to have included St. Louis's Mayor John Darby—watched gleefully as McIntosh and his bright red jacket slowly turned to ash.

ACCORDING TO HIS FRIEND AND LAW PARTNER, WILLIAM Herndon, it was the burning of McIntosh that convinced the then twenty-seven-year-old Abraham Lincoln to deliver his first major political address less than two years after the murder. This was not the first episode of mob violence to draw Lincoln's attention, but it was the most savage and the most indicative of a complete breakdown in the rule of law in the still-young nation. Indeed, only the year before in 1835, Mississippians, like so much of America, seemed to be losing their minds. It was during that brutally hot summer when the white citizens of Vicksburg, an up-and-coming town along the Mississippi River, were hanging people—Blacks and whites alike—with shocking indifference. The impetus for that spree of lynchings was a purported slave insurrection thought to be spawned by the white gamblers of the city's red-light district where Blacks, whites, and a newly decadent culture of sin freely mixed. The Mississippi "excitement," as it was sometimes called, grew beyond the state's borders, as fears of Black insurrections spread like wildfire across the country. Still, from the vantage point of many in Lincoln's home state of Illinois, the horrific violence could be written off because it happened in Mississippi, a state where extrajudicial killings were hardly novel—and not in the presumably far more sober-minded and cosmopolitan city of St. Louis, which defined the newly emerging western frontier of America. The news out of Vicksburg was shocking, but hardly a surprise. For Lincoln, the stories about McIntosh's murder in Illinois's neighboring state of Missouri were far more alarming.

The period after McIntosh's death saw Lincoln take important steps that would come to define his politics in the years to come. Less than one year after McIntosh's burning, in early 1837, Lincoln, now twenty-eight, was preparing not only to speak out against the growing lawlessness and threats to democracy he saw arising throughout the country, but also to lay the groundwork for his public opposition to slavery. Months after McIntosh's burning, Lincoln began searching around the Illinois Assembly for a man, any man, who would sign off on a statement opposing slavery. The legislature had just issued a statement condemning abolitionism, and Lincoln, still a fresh face in the Illinois Assembly, was looking to counter it. Only five members opposed the antiabolition measure, and Lincoln scurried about seeking allies among this tiny group of legislators who might be willing to go on the record with him. Finding a white man holding office in Illinois, free state though it was, to take a public stand against slavery proved nearly impossible. Only Dan Stone, who had decided not to run for reelection, agreed to join him. Lincoln was literally the only public official in the state willing to attach his name to an antislavery measure—one with no legal authority to do anything against the institution anywhere, mind you—and face the political consequences for doing so. The shocking events out of Vicksburg and St. Louis help to explain why.

By themselves, the murders in Mississippi and Missouri were horrific, to be sure. But they also came at a time when America's founders—those who had fought in the revolution and erected the principles of self-government—were dying off. It was increasingly apparent to Lincoln that, as the founding generation were exiting the stage, Americans were succumbing to the kinds of passions more associated with despotism than with the republicanism they had been gifted. When Lincoln finally brought himself to deliver his first major address in January 1838, it was about the dissolution of democratic ideals. In it, he spoke about the "principles of hate" and "motives of revenge" that were once directed against Great Britain, which were now being directed against fellow Americans. The strong attachments that previously existed toward democratic rule, he said, "must fade, is fading, has faded." In more contemporary language, democracy was becoming "memory holed."

As a practical matter, Lincoln decided to speak out because he felt he needed to make a distinctive mark in his state, one where other rising politicians were sharing their thoughts about America's increasingly fraught republic. Lincoln had his own ambitions, his own interest in political power, and he was not prepared to yield the field to his rivals on the momentous questions facing the still very young nation. Lectures on canals, roads, and the charter of the State Bank in Illinois were no longer sufficient ground for someone looking to grow beyond the confines of the state Assembly. And most remarkably, Lincoln sought to make his mark in a speech that put the murders of African Americans, and those who supported their liberation, in the foreground.

All the same, this first major speech of Lincoln's is not carved in marble anywhere. It is not the subject of a book. Nobody has committed it to memory. It is long, complex, and ornate in ways that belie the simple and lucid language Lincoln would become famous for. But, when read carefully, it's difficult not to be transported from the 1830s to the present moment of national crisis. Moreover, it offers the earliest and best indication of Lincoln's values and core beliefs—the ones that every American from primary school onward has come to know. In short, if you want to understand how and when Lincoln formed his core political values—what drove his mutual love for freedom and self-government—then the Lyceum Address, and the terrible events that gave birth to it, is the place to start.

Yet over the past thirty-five years—eighteen as a teacher of American history in public schools, and seventeen as a political historian—I've discovered how rare it is to find any discussion of Lincoln's first speech of consequence. More often than not, the Lyceum Address, named for the "Young Men's Lyceum"—the group that invited Lincoln to speak at Springfield's Baptist Church on January 27, 1838—draws blank stares or, on occasion, the faintest recognition. Devotees of American political thought in academia have some familiarity with it to be sure, but it has hardly punctured the public consciousness. That said, when we read Lincoln's words with an eye toward Vicksburg, St. Louis, and finally, Alton, Illinois, where the famed white abolitionist Elijah P. Lovejoy was murdered, we can see Lincoln's effort to memorialize not only the victims of those horrific acts, but also the vulnerable democracy Lincoln saw hanging in the balance at the very start of his political career.

IT WAS FREDERICK DOUGLASS WHO SAID THAT "NO MAN CAN say anything that is new of Abraham Lincoln," and Douglass said that in 1876, nearly 150 years ago. People have nevertheless tried. Still, as I grew more familiar with the murders and lawless acts that inspired Lincoln's entrance on the political stage as a man ready to tackle the hardest questions facing America, I became increasingly distressed, not so much about what I learned about Lincoln, but about how few treatments there are that tie Lincoln's emergence as a political force and thinker to the stories he told about the victims of mob violence when delivering his first major speech that cold January night in 1838.

Few discussions of the speech, formally known as "The Perpetuation of Our Political Institutions," delve into the accounts of those hunted down and killed in the three Mississippi River towns Lincoln highlighted in his address. Most who have written about it are far too attentive to Lincoln's use of language rather than his attentiveness to racial justice and its importance to democratic life. Scholars have loved dissecting the speech for its call for a "civil religion," or its eerie premonitions about the rise of an American tyrant. And the Lyceum Address is often combed over for its subtle psychological revelations about Lincoln's own ambitions. Rarely have scholars carefully examined the speech's attentiveness to race and why Lincoln would hit this third rail in Illinois politics so early in his career, when for his colleagues, caution on such matters was the order of the day. Yet, in each instance, the murders on the Mississippi from which this book's title gets its name were motivated by racial fears or hatred. To his eternal credit, Lincoln stared down the barrel of the core threat facing American democracy in his time. So should we.

Saladin Ambar
Philadelphia, PA
March 31, 2025

INTRODUCTION

"Ill Omen Among Us"

The first edition of the Springfield, Illinois, *Sangamo Journal* was published on November 10, 1831, the day before Nat Turner was hanged. Turner was a thirty-year-old enslaved Black preacher in Southampton County, Virginia, who, over the course of several days that August, led the largest and bloodiest slave insurrection in American history. Turner and his band of escaped slaves went from plantation to plantation, killing white men, women, and children by the dozens. Some fifty-five whites were killed in the rebellion. Turner's capture and hanging marked the end of an episode that had both enthralled and terrorized white Americans. Perhaps several hundred Blacks in the South were killed in retaliation. To be sure, whites had lived with the fear of Black insurrection since slavery began, but now, Turner's Rebellion demonstrated the ugliest repercussions for maintaining America's "peculiar institution."

While Lincoln's Illinois was a free state, it bordered two slave states—Kentucky to its south and Missouri to its west. The Ohio River reflected the thin line between slavery and freedom, and the geography of Illinois meant that the state would be at the cross-section of debates, rumors, and politics over the future of slavery. As a former Kentuckian, Lincoln's early biography was representative of a population made up of some who were sympathetic to slaveholders, those who were opposed to slavery, and a great many who loathed "meddlesome" abolitionists. This was what passed for moderation in Illinois. So, as news of the Turner Rebellion wound its way into Illinois, it occasioned little outcry against slavery—and much vitriol toward the growing presence of radical white abolitionists, who were blamed for "stirring up" otherwise happy Blacks. For his part, Lincoln offered no comment on Nat Turner, though the rebellion would not change his views of slavery, which he regarded as an affront to humanity and God's law.

In some ways, white abolitionists were as deeply reviled as Blacks, who were deemed largely incapable of acting alone to produce the kind of broad and complex planning that led to Turner's revolt. That one enslaved Black man could lead such a widespread deadly assault in Virginia, which did not have the kind of large Black presence as places like South Carolina or Mississippi, ran counter to so much of what had been taught about Black intelligence.

Quoting the *Richmond Courier*, the *Sangamo Journal* reported that "a negro girl of about 16 or 17 years of age" testified that she heard Turner hatch his plot "among her master's slaves." The girl's testimony, the *Journal* reported, led to the conviction of at least nine of the twenty-six African Americans accused of participating in the rebellion, half of whom were ultimately hanged. The girl's initial account, at first deemed too weak to produce any convictions, became more acceptable in time, as the need to exact punishment proved overwhelming. As the details of Turner's Rebellion began to become known, the idea of Black political equality with whites was damaged even in free states like Illinois. The liberal solution in Lincoln's time was colonization—the repatriation of newly freed Blacks from America to Africa. (The colonization experiment began with the founding of Liberia in 1822.) The idea that Black and white freedom could coexist was held by only the smallest minority of whites.

Lincoln would not move to Springfield for another six years, but he had undoubtedly been made aware of the Turner Rebellion, given his access to the *Sangamo Journal*, the paper that would become his hometown newspaper years later. In time, Lincoln would come to support the idea of colonization before publicly embracing emancipation with full political rights decades later. Anything more would have been an unimaginable stance for a white politician in Illinois at the time.

The Abraham Lincoln who read about Turner's Rebellion was sufficiently antislavery to fuel the political courage of the man who would later be the only man in the Illinois Assembly to risk speaking out against slavery. But he was not prepared to go further. Today, the conventional view of most Americans is that Lincoln came to his more progressive views on race and abolition by way of his love for the Union. But a better path to understanding Lincoln and what made him the Great Emancipator, rather than the Pragmatic Colonizer, can be found in his early political thought. It reflects not only Lincoln's affinity for the rule of law and disdain for mob violence; it also captures his early support for racial justice.

And the Lyceum Address goes further. It counters not only the kind of narrative of lurking Black violence and betrayal presented in the *Sangamo Journal*'s first printing—it also rejects the underlying white nationalism that finds race traitors abounding in the land. In an early passage, Lincoln condemns those whose fury led to the "process of hanging, from gamblers to negroes, from negroes to white citizens, and from these to strangers; till, dead men were seen literally dangling from the boughs of trees upon every roadside; and in numbers almost sufficient, to rival the native Spanish moss of the country, as a drapery of the forest." It was no small thing for Lincoln to conclude that the murder of Blacks—be they enslaved or free—was just as revolting as those of whites—be they gamblers or law-abiding citizens. This is among the earliest examples of Lincoln's genuine respect for human equality.

That Lincoln early in his career so forcefully opposed the rising vigilantism against the most marginalized groups of his era and then became more politically moderate, especially on questions of race and slavery, suggests that Lincoln as president was more of a man who returned to first principles than one who "evolved" for the sake of Union. When Lincoln at the Lyceum raised his voice against those who murder "gamblers," "Negroes," and "those supposed to be leagued with the Negroes," he was making a prophetic warning not only to avoid national "suicide," as he described it; he was also making a case for the interwoven nature of racial justice with the very essence of democracy. That Lincoln did not keep to this strong stand as his political career advanced is rightly lamented; that he returned to it is too often forgotten. For it was the dark, violent, antidemocratic 1830s that forged the prophetic Lincoln—the man who would ultimately help cleanse the "soiled republican robe" of American democracy, as he would later describe it in an 1854 speech in Peoria.

Seeing Lincoln's early democratic sensibilities tied to justice for vulnerable groups is no easy task, in part because the 1830s has been so honeycombed over with notions of democracy's rise in America that we often fail to see that the very things Lincoln feared coming to pass at the Lyceum were well underway. And, because of historians' love affair with a certain version of Alexis de Tocqueville—and indeed, with Andrew Jackson—we have lost the righteous, indignant Abraham Lincoln of Springfield. It is therefore important to read the times as Lincoln read them, to gaze out over the expanse of this "fairest portion of the earth" as he described it that January evening in 1838, and to experience the terror he saw, even as a free, protected, not-quite-twenty-nine-year-old white man, just coming into his powers.

THERE IS LITTLE DOUBT THAT ABRAHAM LINCOLN'S EARLY political thought was shaped by his experience with Jacksonian democracy—the populist support for the underdog and ordinary American—and with the related rise in white male suffrage. Despite his first party affiliation as a Whig and avowed opponent of President Andrew Jackson, historians have nevertheless been keen to note how Lincoln shrewdly carved out political space for himself as both a Jacksonian "man of the people," as well as a critic of Jackson's authoritarian disposition. As one Lincoln biographer notes, at the time Lincoln declared himself a candidate in 1832 for the Illinois state legislature, Jackson remained popular in the state, although party affiliation among voters remained largely unsettled. All the same, Lincoln's political hero was the compromising Speaker of the House Henry Clay—not the headstrong Jackson.

With the possible exception of Woodrow Wilson, no other president in American history has fallen as precipitously in the rankings of presidents by presidential historians than Andrew Jackson in recent years.[1] But for much of American history,

Jackson remained a widely admired, if not uncontroversial, figure. That admiration had much to do with his association with the expansion of white male suffrage along with institutional changes in the parties that broadened the scope of political participation. The opposition toward his presidency has grown owing to greater familiarity and criticism of his Indian removal policies, his unequivocal support for slavery, and his overall attachment to white supremacy. As Princeton historian Sean Wilentz has written about Jackson's legacy, "For Jackson, legislating the people's will and preserving the Constitution had come to mean advancing the battle against concentrated monied power while quieting the growing tumults over slavery."[2]

While the title of Wilentz's work—*The Rise of American Democracy*—obscures the author's more subtle and critical assessments of Jackson's presidency, it does reflect how the 1830s continues to be associated with democracy's expansion rather than its vulnerabilities. The source of this longstanding view of the decade can be most authoritatively traced to Alexis de Tocqueville and the publication of his *Democracy in America* in 1835. Tocqueville's two volumes, the latter published in 1840, were instant successes and today remain admired by both liberals and conservatives alike, albeit for different reasons. In a word, democracy in Jackson's America translated into *equality* for Tocqueville. "It appears to me beyond doubt that sooner or later we shall arrive, like the Americans, at an almost complete equality of conditions," he wrote with his native France in mind.[3]

The equality of social conditions Tocqueville observed during his nine-month visit to America in 1831 was premised on an indispensable and undemocratic caveat, however—the presence of white supremacy—a point he makes plain in his chapter on "The Future of the Three Races in America."[4] Nevertheless,

Tocqueville's emphasis on social equality (among whites) tended to obfuscate his pessimism on race for his admirers over the years. While Tocqueville held race in America and democracy apart, Lincoln saw the linkages between racial injustice and the threat to democracy as a core dilemma of political life. It was a vital and dreaded feature of what Lincoln described as "an ill omen among us" at the Lyceum. By the time of the Lyceum Address, Lincoln had a decade to assess the fruits of Jacksonian democracy. In the end, he did not see its growth as the defining feature of his times; on the contrary, it was democracy's demise that he brooded over.

Another important element that distinguishes Lincoln and Tocqueville is that they drew different conclusions about this era based on a rich appreciation for the founders of the American republic. Tocqueville interviewed many of the newly disenchanted leaders of an older generation of "representatives of the republican elite" in "the Bronze Age of Jacksonian democracy."[5] These older Americans lamented the descent of the country from the earlier, sober Federalist period, into one of "mob rule." But this, according to Tocqueville, reflected the true nature of the *demos*—the people in their mass and unadulterated form. Lincoln's interpretation of the "mob" however, was rather different. His mob—the one he reviled at the Lyceum—was less defined by class, rank, or privilege. On the contrary, it was characterized by its lawlessness and brutality. The former mob is benevolent in Tocqueville's eyes; the latter, for Lincoln, is increasingly malevolent. Both were made up of free, and presumably newly enfranchised, whites. The aristocracy of the mob, if there can be such a thing, lies in its tendency to create forms of superiority for itself, and nothing quite establishes notions of superiority like race in America.

James Madison, whose ideas Lincoln would grapple with at the Lyceum, famously wrote in the *Federalist Papers* that "had every Athenian citizen been a Socrates, every Athenian assembly would have still been a mob."[6] In this fearful construction, a mob is defined by its numbers and crude representativeness of the people en masse. Lincoln's mob, on the other hand, is defined by its actions, not its makeup; and no act is more defining in this regard than bigoted violence. While Andrew Jackson laid assault to Madison's hyper-elitist fear of representative democracy, it was Lincoln who indeed "cleansed the republican robe" of the founders, at least in word, by discrediting racial violence as anathema to the principles of self-government. That stance was first taken publicly in his Lyceum Address, and it was rooted in reports he received from across the country—a sober reminder that neither class, geography, nor whiteness should serve as a basis for citizenship. Andrew Jackson could support only a fragment of what democracy truly meant. Abraham Lincoln supported it whole cloth.

IF THE AGE OF JACKSON WAS A PERIOD OF RADICAL DEMOCRATIC transformation in America, it was also one increasingly defined by violence. Reliable statistics for the decade are hard to come by. Still, if there is a consensus among historians, the era was marked by a rise of violent crime beginning around 1830. The period of great social equality noted by Tocqueville was one where "at least 70 percent of American cities with a population of twenty thousand or more by 1850 experienced some degree of major disorder in the 1830–1850 period."[7] St. Louis, for example, was still under twenty thousand residents in the 1830s, but it was growing rapidly, more than doubling in size between 1830 and 1840. The city would become representative of the growing vigilantism and overall violence of the period. More broadly, it is the political orientation of nationwide racial violence in America at that time that stands out.

It was a bloody and all-too-brutal decade. The 1830s included Congress's Indian Removal Act (1830) that led to the Trail of Tears. This was followed not long after by the Force Bill, where President Jackson was empowered to use violence, if necessary, to get South Carolina to comply with Congress's tariff bill of 1832. As mentioned earlier, Nat Turner's rebellion in Virginia (1831) led to dozens of violent deaths and many bloody reprisals. With Jackson's rejection of the Supreme Court's recognition of Cherokee land claims in 1832, "manifest destiny" became a rallying cry for white settlement of the west. This westward expansion included the violent settlement of Texas by Anglo colonists, leading to the declaration of the Republic of Texas in 1836. Indeed, democracy's expansion among white males in the 1830s was incentivized by the need to settle western lands. This fostered the expansion of voting rights—but also the westward march of slavery, the violent settlement of Indian territory, and ultimately, of territory which had been Mexico's. As the political scientist Paul Frymer has written of "Tocqueville's sanguine vision," the "coerced resettlement of nearly one hundred thousand Native Americans in the 1830s led to deaths in the many thousands."[8]

The series of murders Lincoln references in his Lyceum Address are suggestive of important subtexts to the rise in violence: a rejection of legal norms that do not comply with racial, religious, or political identities. As another historian has written, "The most common forms of mob violence in the 1830s were the abolitionists and the free black communities that supported them."[9] The author is right to emphasize this point, noting how the Black abolitionist David Walker's radical pamphlet, *Appeal to the Colored Citizens of the World* (1829), sparked such a level of outrage and fear among Southerners and white supremacists that it led to mass censorship efforts of the publication, and possibly cost Walker his life.[10] While Lincoln was no abolitionist in 1838, he could well have left out the grisly murder of the free Black man Francis McIntosh in his speech at the Lyceum and still had ample material to condemn mob violence. By centering McIntosh, Lincoln risked "diluting" his message of anti-vigilantism for his white audience.

William Herndon was Abraham Lincoln's close friend at the time of the Lyceum Address, and both men were members of the organization. Years later, Herndon would become Lincoln's law partner, and ultimately, his biographer. While Lincoln scholars have at times been cautious about Herndon's reliability, his recollections have proven hard to dismiss out of hand.[11] Herndon's views of the Lyceum matter because he ascribes the lynching of McIntosh as the principle motivating factor for Lincoln's speech. "Mr. Lincoln's [Lyceum] speech was brought about by the burning in St. Louis a few weeks before, by a mob, of a negro," Herndon would write nearly fifty years later. "Lincoln took this incident as a sort of text for his remarks."[12]

Unfortunately, far too many historians have been drawn to what the Lyceum Address meant to Lincoln as an orator, rather than for his views on slavery and race. This tendency to view the speech as a point of departure for Lincoln's more evolved and polished style as a rhetorician robs Lincoln—and us—of understanding just how central race was to his assessment of American democracy. In Fred Kaplan's important biography of Lincoln as a writer, for example, there is lengthy discussion of the poet Byron, along with Lincoln's rhetorical style at the

Lyceum—with no mention of race, or the murder of McIntosh, or Elijah P. Lovejoy's murder, let alone the Vicksburg gamblers who were hanged.[13] And, in Garry Wills's magisterial work on the Gettysburg Address, the Lyceum speech is described as "comic," "showy," and "labored."[14] It seems that the return to the Lyceum Address by Lincoln scholars will trail the recently found admiration for the address by journalists, who, moved by the events of January 6, 2021, have found new insights in the Lyceum that many have left on the cutting room floor of history.

Of course, even if we accept Herndon's assessment of Lincoln's chief motive behind his speech, that would only account for his centering the murder of Francis McIntosh—the only victim addressed by name by Lincoln—and the subsequent and related killing of the abolitionist Lovejoy, who spoke out against McIntosh's lynching. But we would still be left with the Vicksburg gamblers—five whites killed on the Fourth of July in 1835, some two and a half years before the Lyceum Address. Lincoln's inclusion of the lynching of the gamblers in his Lyceum speech is critical for two reasons: First, it demonstrates his rejection of the kind of puritanical bigotry foisted against "sinful" outsiders, that has been deeply rooted in the American experience. Second, it reveals Lincoln's sense of fairness, insofar as racial identity alone cannot be the criterion by which society administers justice. The rule of law is only as strong as its ability to hold up for those society has deemed expendable.

What made the whites lynched in Vicksburg, Mississippi, expendable? Before considering the question, it's important to note that there were actually two groups of whites who were lynched in Mississippi. The first were the five professional gamblers; the second were an untold number of whites thought to have participated in, or aided, a Black insurrection in neighboring

Hinds and Madison Counties. As Kenneth S. Greenberg illustrates in his book *Honor & Slavery*, "These simultaneous events seem connected, and yet neither contemporaries nor historians have been able to explain the linkage."[15] Yet Lincoln did connect these two events in Mississippi. Moreover, he linked them to an even wider array of violence to legal norms and basic respect for due process throughout the nation. For the white vigilantes in Vicksburg, the whites they killed were simply sinful opportunists or race traitors.

Part of the reason why contemporary readers of the Lyceum Address might not make the connection between the killing of these groups of white victims is because important details from Lincoln's speech are occasionally, and inexplicably, omitted from the text. Take Harvard historian William E. Gienapp's *This Fiery Trial: The Speeches and Writings of Abraham Lincoln*.[16] The following critical passage from the Lyceum has been excised from Gienapp's book, presumably for the sake of brevity:

> Next, negroes, suspected of conspiring to raise an insurrection, were caught up and hanged in all parts of the State: then, white men, supposed to be leagued with the negroes; and finally, strangers, from neighboring States, going thither on business, were, in many instances subjected to the same fate. Thus went on this process of hanging, from gamblers to negroes, from negroes to white citizens, and from these to strangers; till, dead men were seen literally dangling from the boughs of trees upon every road side; and in numbers almost sufficient, to rival the native Spanish moss of the country, as a drapery of the forest.[17]

The thought that this passage is somehow unimportant to Lincoln's message is confounding, to say the least.

It's fair to say Black historians have tended to hold the Lyceum Address in higher regard than their white colleagues. Henry Louis Gates Jr., for example, has deemed the speech "remarkable," and "prescient," highlighting Lincoln's protestations against the murders of McIntosh and Lovejoy in his edited volume on *Lincoln on Race and Slavery*.[18] Unfortunately, for most, the Lyceum Address seems bifurcated by the worlds of race or rhetoric, with scholars generally unwilling to associate Lincoln's categories of exclusion (the "gamblers," "negroes," and "those leagued with negroes" he speaks of that were murdered) with having much of anything to do with his essential motivations.

Thankfully, the Lyceum Address may just now be emerging from the historical haze that has weighed it down. The myths of Tocquevillian equality, Jacksonian democratization, and the sometimes backhanded appreciation of the speech only for its association with Lincoln's "inferior" phase of rhetoric, would be difficult enough to overcome. But there is another myth that Lincoln punctures at the Lyceum, one that needs addressing—the myth of the Midwest.

The killing of McIntosh is sometimes referred to as "America's first lynching."[19] While a statement impossible to verify, McIntosh's murder did set in motion a series of influential events, beginning with the condemnation of his killing by Lovejoy. Lovejoy visited the horrific remains of McIntosh the next day, writing that the agony and moral calamity of what he and others witnessed was so great that "out of bitterness of heart," they "prayed that they might not live."[20] It was Lovejoy's writings on McIntosh's killing that led to his being harried out of St. Louis by pro-slavery mobs, forcing his relocation to the nearby free city of Alton, Illinois, in July of 1836. Indeed, Lovejoy had been targeted by name by Judge Luke E. Lawless, who presided over the grand jury hearing of those to be charged with McIntosh's killing. Lawless blamed Lovejoy's abolitionist writings for inciting McIntosh to violence. No one was ultimately charged with McIntosh's murder. But on November 7, 1837, Lovejoy was murdered and his printing press was tossed into the Mississippi River, as another white mob pursued its own form of justice.

When thinking of this sort of mob violence, invariably we are tempted to think of these killings as "Southern" in both place and nature. They are not the sort of crimes often associated with the Midwest. But as historians such as Walter Johnson and Michael J. Pfeifer have shown, nothing could be further from the truth.[21] Indeed, "the origins of American lynching can best be understood as a national, indeed, a transnational process of cultural and legal formation."[22] Lincoln's formative experiences in New Salem, Illinois—a town settled by "roughs and bullies"—involved its share of fistfights and more than its share of wrestling.[23] Proving one's toughness on what was still the frontier was integral, even as the broader encroachment on Indian lands led to wider and bloodier conflict, such as the Black Hawk War, in which Lincoln was briefly engaged. Indeed, it was the Black Hawk War that gave the federal government the most proximate impetus for its Indian Removal policy under Andrew Jackson. More to the point, Lincoln goes to pains in his Lyceum Address to argue that the rise in mob violence and general lawlessness is a national phenomenon.

Lincoln rose to prominence in America's western frontier—today's Midwest. To what extent were his earliest views with respect to race cultivated in New Salem and in Springfield?

The temptation to ignore Lincoln's earliest opposition to white supremacy is strong, given his long-held opposition to abolition. Take Eric Foner's highly acclaimed and excellent work on Lincoln and slavery. At one point, Foner writes, "Race is our obsession, not Lincoln's. Other than in 1857–58, this was not a subject to which he devoted much attention before the Civil War."[24] Foner points to Lincoln's casual racism as well as his opposition over his career in politics to Black civil rights, and he is correct in doing so. But he also peremptorily counters this notion earlier in his book, when he assesses the Lyceum Address. Noting that Lincoln addresses the "mulatto" McIntosh by name (Lovejoy, who is white, goes unnamed by Lincoln), while providing important and gruesome details about his murder, Foner makes the point that Lincoln somehow *was*, in fact, interested in race. "Given the pervasiveness of mob violence in the 1830s, Lincoln did not have to choose black victims to illustrate his point. His subtext was that slavery created a social environment that encouraged lawlessness."[25]

Foner never ventures into why Lincoln *did* make race a vital part of the Lyceum speech. Perhaps because Lincoln was a racist, albeit a conventional one for the times, Foner is loath to credit Lincoln for expressing an outlying sentiment at the Lyceum. Here is where the complexities of race work their intellectual mischief. The possibility that Lincoln held conflicting beliefs about African Americans is not all that surprising—least of all to African Americans. That he was most likely a garden variety believer in white supremacy while also opposed to extrajudicial violence against Blacks, would place him in a moderate to progressive camp of racialists for his time—including a good number of abolitionists. That he offered such strong condemnations of McIntosh's killing and explicitly linked it to the erosion of democratic values was unique for someone who was not a committed abolitionist. Why then?

Lincoln's motives were not simply political, but prophetic, meaning they were stirred by a selfless and moral desire to warn the nation that it was poised for destruction—one of its own making. Any effort to reverse-engineer Lincoln's transformation as a political thinker on the question of slavery should proceed with caution. But the effort should be made, and once attempted, Lincoln's speech "On the Perpetuation of Our Political Institutions" must be the starting point. Until very recently, I would have agreed with Foner's assessment of Lincoln: "If Lincoln achieved greatness, he grew into it."[26] In an elemental way, this must be true, as it is true for nearly every leader. But perhaps it was the greater truth for Lincoln as it is for others who lose their way and then return to themselves. Our growth is as often occasioned by a restoration of who we are, as it is by an evolution. We may have Lincoln wrong, after all. If we take Lincoln's earliest public speech seriously, then we may reach a very different conclusion about the leader he became. Abraham Lincoln did not grow into greatness. He reclaimed it.

THIS BOOK TAKES ITS OUTLINE FROM THE LYNCHINGS Lincoln highlighted in his Lyceum Address. I begin in chapter one ("Unraveling") with the story of the five white gamblers murdered in Vicksburg, Mississippi—a river town whose growth and infusion of outsiders marked it out as a "Gomorrah" of the West. The horrendous tale is among the lesser-known stories associated with the Lyceum speech, even among Lincoln aficionados. Even more obscure is the second group of whites killed in Mississippi—those associated with a purported Black insurrection in neighboring counties. In the parlance of contemporary white supremacists, these "race traitors" posed as great a threat to white rule as their enslaved Black charges. For all the research on the Lyceum that sees Lincoln's speech as but one of a series of addresses concerned with mob violence at the time, it is Lincoln's speech that stands alone for connecting the fears of Black rebellion and moral decline with racial treason. It is an astounding connection, and Lincoln's prescience can only be fully appreciated if the story of what took place in Vicksburg in 1835 is told.

In chapter two ("Failing"), I address the burning of Francis McIntosh and why Lincoln's detailed account of his murder matters for understanding his early political thought. For it was McIntosh's killing—one that calls to mind the murder of Emmett Till—that galvanized the forces of abolition like no other. Indeed, in chapter three ("Searching"), I take on the killing of Elijah P. Lovejoy, who fled St. Louis for Alton, Illinois, to avoid the vengeful wrath of whites who viewed his condemnation of McIntosh's murder as treasonous. These lynchings have an interconnectedness important to drawing out the special qualities embedded in Lincoln's Lyceum Address and his early political thought. Lovejoy's murder would only lead to further intensification of the abolitionist cause—and for Lincoln, illuminate the dire state of American democracy at the time.

In chapter four ("Transformation"), I move on to a full reflection on the Lyceum Address as not only an important touchstone for understanding Lincoln's rhetorical style, but more importantly, as a speech that in many ways is a precursor to his Second Inaugural Address, delivered twenty-seven years later. For it was in the Second Inaugural that Lincoln warned the nation of the

Almighty's divine justice for the sin of slavery; at the Lyceum, it was a warning against national suicide. The United States was suffering from a form of political malady that had rendered it mad—and that madness was leading toward self-immolation. The "suicide" Lincoln prophesied was, of course, the Civil War. That he would later attribute the war to divine judgment does not take away from the Lyceum Address as his first jeremiad—one in which Lincoln hoped the invocation of a civil religion for the nation might forestall disaster.

In chapter five ("Fortifications"), I address the history of the Lyceum Address and how scholars and citizens alike have viewed Lincoln's early political thought. And I detail how and why the Lyceum has become, like Washington or Eisenhower's Farewell Address, a proverbial alarm for national awakening—in Lincoln's case, for the need to heal the soul of a people deeply attached to racial hatred and the easy path of authoritarianism. These twin character flaws, embedded in the political psyche of America, have come home to roost in recent years, unlike any other time since the Civil War.

In each of the forthcoming chapters, I position Lincoln's personal struggles alongside his political considerations. Indeed, one cannot fully separate the personal from the political Lincoln—and this is likely the case for all political figures of consequence. Still, this is especially so for Lincoln, as his late twenties proved to be the period where his personal and political aspirations and inner trials intersected profoundly for the first time.

As America's recent political tribulations attest, it is well past time to heed Lincoln's warning issued at the Lyceum. But to do so, we must first return to the events that moved Lincoln as a young politician in Springfield, Illinois. And we must resist the temptation to assess the Lyceum Address as simply a starting point for understanding Lincoln's gifts as a rhetorician. We must see it for the dark, prophetic, and civil sermon on race and democracy that it was—a speech that defined Lincoln and his beliefs for decades to come.

ONE

1835: UNRAVELING

The early summer of 1835 in Madison County, Mississippi, was a cruel one. From "mid-May to mid-July," the sky was said to have been uninterrupted by a single clear day. The rain was unrelenting with the cotton yield predicted to be desperately small. The enslaved Black population of the county, who outnumbered whites nearly three to one, were mostly idle because of the downpours, unable to satisfy the needs of the formerly flush white planter community, now facing a lost cotton harvest and a banking panic already a year in the making.[1]

Cotton made Mississippi. In 1820, ten million pounds were produced in the Magnolia State. By 1834, production had risen to eighty-five million pounds.[2] Now, suddenly, all stood to be lost. This unsettling of the natural order would be followed by a series of manmade terrors that would envelop Madison, and then the rest of Mississippi, before dying out near Christmastime, with the violence traveling as far east as Washington.[3] Within a few years, the hysteria would become the subject of a novel.[4]

It began with a whisper. In late June, a widowed white woman named Mrs. Latham, living in Madison's tiny neighborhood of

Beattie's Bluff, told her son Lorenzo she had overheard several of her slaves planning an insurrection "to kill all the whites."[5] The rumor conjured up another Turner-like nightmare, now a staple of Southern white fears. Slave rebellions were always plausible in the American South, but fears of them had grown particularly acute—especially in counties such as Madison, where whites were a distinct minority.[6]

Surprised by the new and uncharacteristic "insolent and disobedient" behavior among her slaves, Mrs. Latham grew suspicious of their "mysterious" conduct. While eavesdropping on two of her Black wet nurses, she overheard one of her "girls" tell another that "she wished to God it was all over and done with; that she was tired of waiting on the *white folks*, and wanted to be her own mistress the balance of her days, and clean her own house."[7] From this declaration, the conversation grew more ominous, with the same woman later telling an enslaved man, "Is it not a pity to kill such—!" The unspoken subject of the sentence was the small white child in the woman's care.

After learning of the plot from his mother, Lorenzo Latham interrogated the slaves in question, confirming the pledge to kill the small child, along with a larger plan to "kill all the whites." Once informed by Mr. Latham, a "vigilance" committee meeting was held in nearby Livingston, Mississippi, on June 27, where several slaves and their white plantation owners were questioned by "a large and respectable meeting of the citizens." A week had passed since widow Latham's claims were made known, with the lack of urgency to convene quickly casting some doubt on her veracity. Nevertheless, a number of Blacks queried in Livingston from neighboring plantations were tortured—or "severely chastised" in the language of the white slave owners in Madison—and soon confessed to some elements of a planned slave uprising.

Among the decisions reached at the Livingston meeting was to establish slave "patrols" that would gather information and report back to the group a few days later on June 30.

It was at that meeting that an "old Negro" was brought in, having been accused of asking one of the slaves interrogated at Livingston for "powder and shot" for the purpose of killing whites. Denying any knowledge of a conspiracy, he was subsequently whipped until "he confessed all he knew respecting the contemplated insurrection." Other Blacks were brought in over the ensuing days and similarly tortured, although not all to the point of confession, with one accused slave saying they "might whip on until they killed him."

Still, the committee concluded that a slave insurrection was indeed planned; that it was to take place on the Fourth of July, when Blacks could freely congregate and whites would be distracted. Any and all "ringleaders" of the uprising were to be "hanged in order to strike terror among the rest, and by that means crush all hopes of their freedom." July 2 was agreed upon as the date for administering the executions. But another more insidious task for the Livingston committee remained.

Since news of the insurrection had first surfaced, speculation arose that the whites of Madison "were not to contend alone with a few daring and desperate negroes . . . but that these negroes were instigated and encouraged by some of the most wicked and abandoned *white men* in the country; highway robbers, murderers, and abolitionists, who were to supply them with arms and ammunition, and lead them on to the work of massacre and carnage, conflagration and blood." The prospect of white race traitors siding with Black slaves in an insurrection underscored the vulnerability and paranoia felt on large, isolated plantations by white slave owners. Confronting the likely prospect of having to administer swift and extralegal justice upon white citizens found guilty of conspiring with Blacks, meant having to justify circumventing the rule of law, along with the rights and privileges with which whites were customarily entitled. And so, a "Committee of Safety" was established at Livingston, authorizing its members to "carry into effect any order which the committee might make . . . for the safety of the community."

As it turned out, Mrs. Latham's fear of a Black insurrection was stoked not only by what she was thought to have heard from her slaves in Beattie's Bluff. Months before, a pamphlet began circulating throughout Mississippi warning in great detail of just such an uprising. The document told the story of a fanatical white leader whose plans included not only the decimation of Mississippi's whites, but those on plantations as far south as New Orleans. An entire race war was in the making. Moreover, the pamphlet revealed that it was not only those outcasts from polite society who were enlisted in the effort—the highway robbers, murderers, and abolitionists were cited in the proceedings at Livingston. There was another despised group of immoral charlatans who were part of the conspiracy. Their crooked nature and vile manners were well known throughout the state, as they plied their craft in the wealthy and increasingly decadent town of Vicksburg, along the bluffs of the Mississippi River, some fifty miles from Livingston. These were the river city's gamblers, who, on the Fourth of July, would play a tragic role in one of the great and ignominious stories of racial terror in the long history of American slavery.

• • •

SIX HUNDRED MILES UP THE MISSISSIPPI RIVER THAT AUGUST, Abraham Lincoln, by all accounts, was losing his mind. A deep, grief-filled depression led those around him to fear he was suicidal. But his mental state had nothing to do with the news coming out of Vicksburg. What had begun as an auspicious year with great personal and political promise had morphed into one filled with unspeakable sorrow for the young politician from New Salem.

The year began quietly enough, with Lincoln several weeks into his first session in the Illinois General Assembly, held in the capital of Vandalia. The short session ran from December 1,1834, through February 13, 1835. Having been elected to the Assembly on August 4 after a failed campaign in 1832, Lincoln had a few months to enjoy his victory before taking office. More important, this was the period when, at the urging of his friend John Todd Stuart, Lincoln began to study the law. Lincoln knew the highly educated and distinguished Stuart from their time together in the Black Hawk War, that conflict between the United States government and the Black Hawk nation over disputed territory in Illinois and what would later become Wisconsin. During the war, Lincoln made a lasting impression upon Stuart. After the war, Stuart observed that his friend's defeat in the 1832 election actually enhanced his reputation. "Lincoln in this race, although he was defeated, acquired a reputation for candor and honesty, as well as for ability in speech-making. He made friends everywhere he went—he ran on the square—and thereby acquired the respect and confidence of everybody."[8]

"Every man is said to have his peculiar ambition," Lincoln wrote in declaring his candidacy. "Whether it be true or not, I can say for one that I have no other so great as that of being truly esteemed of my fellow men, by rendering myself worthy of their esteem. How far I shall succeed in gratifying this ambition, is yet to be developed."[9] Now, more than two years later, he'd get his chance to demonstrate his worthiness. At the very least, he'd be able to draw a consistent salary as an assemblyman.

Lincoln's early days in government were marked by financial hardships. For several years in New Salem, he co-owned a fledgling supply store with William Berry. When Berry died suddenly in January of 1835, Lincoln was left with just over one thousand dollars of debt. Having bought the store on credit, the failed business would bedevil Lincoln until 1848, when the account—jokingly referred to by Lincoln as "the national debt"—was finally paid off.[10] As George Close, who worked long hard hours with Lincoln as a day laborer just before he moved to New Salem, put it: Lincoln "*had nothing, only plenty of friends.*"[11]

Lincoln earned a reputation for toughness and honesty early on in New Salem. The wild-haired, tall, and gangly youth with mercurial grayish-blue eyes made quite an impression, with "his strange clothes and uncouth awkwardness advertising him."[12] Arriving on his own in New Salem after leaving his father in nearby Decatur in 1831, Lincoln stood out for more than just his six-foot-four-inch frame and unusual appearance. Uncommon for the time, he flaunted his rejection of most every dearly held orthodox convention of the Baptist church, earning a reputation as an infidel.

Lincoln's religious views were so unpopular that a friend burned an anti-Christian tract Lincoln had written before it could see the light of day. Lincoln's friend John Hill "snatched it from Lincoln's hand, when Lincoln was not expecting it, and ran it into an old-fashioned ten-plate [*sic*] stove, heated as hot as a furnace; and so Lincoln's book went up to the clouds in smoke."[13] Like Jefferson and other American founders, Lincoln gravitated toward deism and an enlightened questioning of biblical truths.[14] But America was in a period of religious awakening now, and that school of thought became outdated. This was a time of Christian revivals marked by a temperance movement, the push for women's rights, and abolitionism. Despite his early controversial religious views, Lincoln won over far more admirers than he lost in New Salem, and it was a testament to his personal integrity and affability that he was embraced so broadly by members of the community.

Politically, Lincoln hewed closely to the Whig line in American politics. He abhorred slavery but was antiabolitionist; he was opposed to Andrew Jackson, but mindful not to flaunt it in a state where Jackson remained quite popular. And he was very much a conventional local politician, concerned with issues affecting his district and county. In his declaration of candidacy back in 1832, he began by explaining that his service would be in keeping with both custom and "the true principles of republicanism," perhaps his earliest public nod to his love of representative government.[15] He then expressed his support for "the public utility of internal improvements," a Whig position extolling the national benefits of infrastructure ("the opening of good roads, and in the clearing of navigable streams.").[16] It was the Whig party that was aligned with national issues and government—roads, the national bank, and the like—while Democrats fought for local issues and what would later be called states' rights. True to his political brand, Lincoln was hoping to benefit his rural frontier district by creating greater connectivity to the burgeoning national economy linked by rivers, railroads, and canals. his rural frontier district by creating greater connectivity to the burgeoning national economy linked by rivers, railroads, and canals. After a lengthy discussion of the particulars of his wonkish expertise such as "calculations with regard to the navigation of the Sangamo [River]," and the cost of financing public works projects, Lincoln then expressed his support for public education and its moral value.[17] Whatever his personal religious views, Lincoln quickly learned that in office, he had to reflect the interests and sentiments of his constituents.

Next, Lincoln stated his inclination to uphold those laws already in place—a modest and conservative promise to "not [meddle]" with laws passed by others, unless there was sufficient public support for doing so.[18] This early indicator of Lincoln's reverence for the law reflected his broader understanding of constitutional government. That which is legally binding upon a people ought to be adhered to—and to do otherwise, would be to undermine the foundations of society. Lincoln from the outset was no radical predisposed to revisiting the laws of prior generations; nor was he like Henry David Thoreau, the great transcendentalist who reserved for himself and those of conscience the right to disobey the laws that ran contrary to one's innate sense of right.

At the end of his first session in the General Assembly in February 1835, Lincoln had only modest accomplishments to boast of. He was quiet, passing a toll bill and offering his support for a number of public works projects. He mostly followed the lead of his friend Stuart, voting with him frequently, while keeping a low profile. Notably, Lincoln did forge a relationship with the influential *Sangamo Journal* in Springfield during this time, one that would become an early outlet for his opinions on politics, as he would, by some accounts, write hundreds of anonymous editorials for them over the years.[19]

The world of politics was opening up for Lincoln in the early months of 1835. It was a humble beginning to be sure, but he was positioning himself for greater things. And he was in the early part of the year, drawn to other, more personal motivations that would shape his life—and induce, in part, the psychic trauma of August. As his first legislative session was in its final days, only those closest to Lincoln knew that he was deeply in love with a vivacious twenty-two-year-old Kentucky-born woman named Ann Rutledge, whom he was hoping to marry.

THE PEOPLE OF NEW SALEM FIRST BECAME ACQUAINTED with Abraham Lincoln in the spring of 1831, when the twenty-two-year-old stranger, newly emancipated from his father, set out on a flatboat for New Orleans to sell goods and, by accident, became lodged in the Sangamon River and needed assistance. A self-described "piece of floating driftwood," Lincoln made quite an appearance in the small town as he and his flatboat mates, John Hanks and John D. Johnston, tried to rescue the boat and its cargo, with Lincoln's "pants rolled up to his knees and shirt wet with sweat and combing his fuzzie hair with his fingers as he pounded away on the boat."[20] Impressed by Lincoln's uncanny ingenuity in salvaging the boat, Denton Offutt, who had financed the New Orleans trip, promised Lincoln a position as manager of a store in New Salem upon his return.[21] Later that July, Lincoln returned to the small village to make good on Offutt's promise. But Offutt's store was not quite ready, and Lincoln had to scramble, working hand-to-mouth until the store was finally ready in September.[22]

Lincoln's early days in New Salem were marked by the impression he made for both his physical and intellectual talents. He famously got in with a gang of roughnecks from nearby Clary's Grove and proved his toughness as a wrestler. And he likewise earned high marks for his skills in New Salem's debating club, founded by James Rutledge, who owned the tavern where Lincoln, for a time, would room and board.[23] It was at Rutledge's tavern where Lincoln first met Rutledge's then-eighteen-year-old daughter, Ann.

Ann was one of the brightest students of New Salem's respected teacher, Mentor Graham. Graham, who would go on to tutor Lincoln for a time, was struck by Ann's "quick mind." A foot shorter than Lincoln, Ann was about five-foot-four and 125 pounds, with auburn or reddish blonde hair, large blue eyes, and a "well-made, beautiful" mouth.[24] Her striking appearance coupled with her intellect and cultured manners drew numerous male admirers.

By the time Lincoln expressed romantic interest in her, Rutledge had already turned down two serious suitors and was entertaining a third. Lincoln had spent some time getting to know Ann.[25] This would pass for high flirtation for Lincoln, who, despite an abiding inner passion for women, was almost always baffled in their presence.

If Lincoln's early relationship with women could be boiled down to a single word, it would be "awkward." Whether his discomfort in the presence of women—particularly young women—was attributable to his self-consciousness over his appearance, lack of social graces, or sheer fright, Lincoln gained a swift reputation for a general lack of interest in women—at least in terms of a willingness to publicly engage with them.[26] "[W] omen are the only things that cannot hurt me that I am afraid of," Lincoln would later admit.[27] As one fellow boarder at the tavern in New Salem remembered, "while we boarded at this Tavern there came a family Containing an old Lady her Son and Three stylish Daughters from the State of Virginia and stopped their for 2 or 3 weeks and during there stay I do not remember of Mr Lincoln Ever eating at the same table when they did."[28]

Besides "awkward," the other recurring descriptor employed when recalling Lincoln's romantic life—or lack thereof—is "homely." Yet, young Lincoln did not eschew the company of women altogether. He seemed comfortable in the company of older women, where he felt at ease and less self-conscious of his manners and appearance.[29] And Lincoln displayed early interest and common youthful passions for women, dating to his life in Indiana.[30] There is also good reason to believe that Lincoln found an outlet for his sexual passions common to frontier life for young men at the time—prostitution.

Perhaps as early as his time in the Black Hawk War in 1832, and later during the height of his mental anguish in late 1835, and finally, around 1839, Lincoln likely visited prostitutes—with each distinct episode reflecting different aspects of Lincoln's station in life. That Lincoln and Joshua Speed as soldiers went to "the hoar houses" in Galena, Illinois, during the war, as Speed told William Herndon years later, is hardly shocking given the history of life away from home during military campaigns.[31] In 1839, it was said that Lincoln saw a prostitute recommended to him by Speed. Embarrassed, Lincoln dressed after realizing he was two dollars short of what the woman charged. Refusing to "go on credit" as he put it, he offered to pay her what he had anyway.[32] Intriguing as these encounters may be, it was Lincoln's experience after his ill-fated relationship with Ann Rutledge that contributed to his deteriorating mental state.[33]

Sometime in early 1835, after returning from his legislative session in February, Lincoln and Rutledge became engaged.[34] The engagement was kept quiet for two possible reasons. The first was Ann's superstition that "engagements made too far [ahead] sometimes failed," and this would necessarily be a lengthy one, as Lincoln needed to first complete his legal studies.[35] The other, more complicated reason was that Rutledge was already spoken for. The third suitor Rutledge turned down was one John McNeil—"the catch of the village"—a successful merchant, who mysteriously remained away in New York for some three years, ostensibly to bring his family to New Salem. Despairing of his return, Ann wanted to break off her engagement with McNeil honorably, before announcing any new matrimonial plans.[36] Further clouding McNeil's prospects was that, in 1833, he revealed to Ann that John McNamar was his real name, telling her he kept his true identity a secret to keep any money-seeking New York relatives at bay until his financial situation was more secure.[37]

The revelation created understandable skepticism in the Rutledge family. Ultimately, Lincoln's courtship proved to have greater resonance with Ann. As Ann's sister Nancy put it, Lincoln "declared his love and was accepted for she loved him with a more and enduring affection than she ever felt for McNamar."[38] Given the awkward and unsettling backstory to their romance, it makes some sense that no letters survive between Lincoln and Rutledge. Any revelation of their relationship would have likely undermined both their reputations—at least until the McNamar proposal was spurned or withdrawn.

THE SAME UNRELENTING RAIN THAT BEFELL MADISON County in Mississippi in the summer of 1835 also afflicted New Salem. The rains "contributed to a record mosquito crop, and outbreaks of malaria followed."[39] The heat was equally intense—"the hottest [summer] ever known in Illinois"—according to a medical thesis published the following year.[40] Sometime in early August, Rutledge grew weary to the point of exhaustion and became too weak to get out of bed.[41] The downpours likely flooded the family well and contaminated the Rutledges' drinking water. Ann "burned all over," except for her feet, which were warmed with hot stones.[42] The likely culprit was typhoid fever, diagnosed at the time as "brain fever."

Determined to see Ann, Lincoln attempted to visit her one rainy evening, stopping at the cabin of Parson John M. Barry, who persuaded the despondent Lincoln to stay the night. Lincoln agreed, but got no rest, pacing the floor until the next morning.[43] "Out of her head," in a state of delirium days before she died, Ann was in and out of consciousness, when at last she "called for Abe."[44] When he reached her, they spoke briefly together, a final meeting marked by mutual tears, as the heavy-hearted Lincoln, leaving the room, "stopped at the door and looked back."[45]

Ann Rutledge died on August 25, 1835. "I can never be reconciled to have the snow, rains, and storms to beat on her grave," Lincoln would say.[46] Three years to the date of her death, an anonymous poem was published on page two in the *Sangamo Journal*.[47] However unidentified, there can be little doubt as to who the author was, given the grim nature of the anniversary.

THE SUICIDE'S SOLILOQUY

The following lines were said to have been found near the bones of a man supposed to have committed suicide, in a deep forest, on the flat branch of the Sangamon, some time ago.

Here, where the lonely hooting owl
Sends forth his midnight moans,
Fierce wolves shall o'er my carcase growl,
Or buzzards pick my bones.
No fellow-man shall learn my fate,
Or where my ashes lie;
Unless by beasts drawn round their bait,
Or by the ravens' cry.
Yes! I've resolved the deed to do,
And this the place to do it:
This heart I'll rush a dagger through,
Though I in hell should rue it!
Hell! What is hell to one like me
Who pleasures never knew;
By friends consigned to misery,
By hope deserted too?
To ease me of this power to think,
That through my bosom raves,
I'll headlong leap from hell's high brink,
And wallow in its waves.
Though devils yell, and burning chains
May waken long regret;

Their frightful screams, and piercing pains,
Will help me to forget.
Yes! I'm prepared, through endless night,
To take that fiery berth!
Think not with tales of hell to fright
Me, who am damn'd on earth!
Sweet steel! come forth from your sheath,
And glist'ning, speak your powers;
Rip up the organs of my breath,
And draw my blood in showers!
I strike! It quivers in that heart
Which drives me to this end;
I draw and kiss the bloody dart,
My last—my only friend!

It was about the time Ann Rutledge fell ill that the *Sangamo Journal* published two articles about the bloody scenes in Mississippi. The first, published on July 25 under the headline "Mobs at Vicksburg," recounted how "the steamboat Majestic" arrived at Vicksburg from New Orleans to find the town in a "state of great excitement, occasioned by the outrages of a lawless mob upon the gamblers who were assembled there."[48] The story noted that, at a meeting held on Saturday, July 4, Vicksburg citizens voted to give the city's gamblers "twenty-four-hours' notice" to leave the city. Some hundred notices were soon plastered around the town as fair warning. Years later, as the lynching spree grew in fame, so too did the value of the notices: some were auctioned off for one hundred dollars or more as late as 1950.[49]

Notice.

AT a meeting of the citizens of Vicksburg on Saturday the 4th day of July, it was

***Resolved*, That a notice be given to all *professional* GAMBLERS, that the citizens of Vicksburg are resolved to exclude them from this place and its vicinity, and that *twenty-four hours* notice be given them to leave the place.**

***Resolved*, That all persons permitting Faro dealing in their houses, be also notified, that they will be prosecuted therefor.**

***Resolved*, That one hundred copies of the foregoing resolutions be printed and stuck up at the corners of the streets, and the publication be deemed notice.**

***Vicksburg*, *July* 5, 1835.**

Vicksburg notice to gamblers, July 5, 1835, Mississippi Dept. of Archives and History.

The gamblers were vigorously pursued, with five or six discovered barricaded in a house the following day. The mob that had assembled proceeded to "demolish [the] house," even as one of the gamblers inside fired upon the crowd, killing "a citizen, Dr. [Hugh] Bodley." As the *Journal* reported, "This so enraged the populace that, as soon as they secured their victims, they proceeded to execute summary vengeance upon them. The five or six taken were forth with shot, or hung, without any regard to law, and the bodies of the latter suffered to remain in this position for twenty-four hours." The names recorded of the first five hanged were "North, Hullams, Dutch Bill, Smith, and McCall.

Their bodies were cut down on the morning after their execution and buried in a ditch," according to a report in the *Vicksburg Register*.[50]

The *Sangamo Journal*'s account noted that "the excesses did not stop here: operations were extended to divers suspected persons in the neighborhood, wherever they could be found, until it is conjectured, fifteen or twenty lives were taken. A part of this number, however, were slaves who had been engaged in some rebellious disturbances, excited, as is said, by the gamblers."[51] Dozens, perhaps hundreds, of Blacks and whites were ultimately killed in the days after, a death count lost to history. But what did Vicksburg's small community of white gamblers have to do with the enslaved Blacks of Mississippi?

The *Journal*'s second, even more ominous article ("Insurrection of Slaves in Mississippi") of August 1 answered the question. It cited a merchant from Nashville who received a letter from a "gentleman of some respectability" in Mississippi, claiming that "an insurrection, has, it appears, been on hand among the negroes for the last six months, headed by white-men."[52] Vicksburg's gamblers, an already shunned group, were easy targets to implicate in the alleged rebellion. An important part of the reporting concerned white Mississippians' fierce opposition to miscegenation—the dreaded fear of interracial mixing. "It appears from a confession," the *Journal* continued, that the multiracial rebellion's "route was to have commenced from some place above [Madison County] and proceed thence through the principle [*sic*] towns of Natchez, and then on to New Orleans, murdering all the white men and ugly women—sparing the handsome ones and making wives of them—and plundering and burning as they went."[53] It was, in short, a nightmare of white racial anxieties: Black men forcibly marrying the most beautiful white women, killing their husbands and children, all the while being aided by amoral and disloyal white men.

The self-righteous zealotry that drove the lynchings at Vicksburg—the first murders in the trio Lincoln would cite in his Lyceum Address—and its surrounding environs was a powerful force behind the premise that the mob, rather than courts, were justified in administering their own form of justice. Today, a memorial erected to Dr. Bodley in 1837 stands as the oldest monument in Vicksburg. Its inscription reads: "Erected by a grateful community to the memory of Dr. Hugh Bodley, Murdered by the gamblers July 5, 1835, while defending the morals of Vicksburg." No such memorial exists to those Blacks lynched in the ensuing days, nor the gamblers or others engulfed in the killing frenzy.

The neighborhood where the killing spree began was the old "kangaroo" district of Vicksburg, named after a brothel, found in the westernmost section of the city. The kangaroo district begat its share of "kangaroo courts"—the origin of our American vernacular expression for rigged courts—so named because "extralegal" punishment of Vicksburg's Blacks, gamblers, and prostitutes was permissible there.[54] It was thus Mississippi's explosive cocktail of sin, race, and hearsay that set off the conflagration that was to begin in Vicksburg. But that cocktail was mixed earlier in the year by the pamphlet mentioned at the start of this chapter—the one that likely moved Madison County's widow Latham to suspect her slaves of plotting to "kill all the whites."

The pamphlet, circulated in the spring of 1835, linked enslaved African Americans to the murder of the Vicksburg gamblers. The author was one Virgil A. Stewart, who, adopting the pseudonym "August Q. Walton," wrote one of the great false and conspiratorial pamphlets in American history. Stewart's pamphlet reads today like an antebellum "Protocols of the Elders of Zion"—the infamous conspiratorial fabrication alleging Jewish global dominance first published in Russia in 1903. Stewart's pamphlet accused John A. Murrell, a petty horse thief and swindler of the West, with organizing a slave rebellion designed to imperil the South, all under the aegis of a shadowy cabal known as "the Mystic Clan." No substantive proof of the plot has ever been uncovered, and Stewart's story has been debunked as "flagrantly absurd."[55] No matter. As we have seen in our own politics today, the publication of repeated lies, asserted with unwavering certainty, remains a powerful tool for those seeking a politics of racial purity.

Stewart's pamphlet's endlessly descriptive title told the story—say it in one breath if you can: "A history of the detection, conviction, life and designs of John A. Murell, the great western land pirate: together with his system of villany, and plan of exciting a Negro rebellion; also, a catalogue of the names of four hundred and fifty-five of the mystic clan fellows and followers, and a statement of their efforts for the destruction of Virgil A. Stewart, the young man who detected him; to which is added a biographical sketch of V. A. Stewart."[56] Stewart traveled far and wide promoting his pamphlet, giving public lectures about the "Mystic Clan" and the pending insurrection throughout the spring of 1835. It was the lecture he delivered in June "to the citizens of Madison County, Mississippi, deep in the plantation country northeast of Vicksburg," that sparked the panic among plantation owners.[57]

While Lincoln did not move to Springfield until 1837 when the *Sangamo Journal* story of the Vicksburg gamblers appeared, as someone who read and wrote for the *Journal*, he most certainly heard of it. Word of the conspiracy and Stewart's "Mystic Clan" spread throughout the South and Midwest like wildfire, along with the legend of John Murrell. Decades later, Mark Twain would write about Murrell (spelled "Murel" in his account) in his memoir *Life on the Mississippi*. In his account, Twain presented the "Murrell Excitement" of his youth as more fact than fiction, including Stewart's allegation of a joint Black and white conspiracy to take New Orleans. Comparing Murrell to the famed outlaw Jesse James, Twain rhapsodized: "James was a retail rascal," Twain wrote. "Murel, wholesale. James' modest genius dreamed of no loftier flight than the planning of raids upon cars, coaches, and country banks; Murel projected negro insurrections and the capture of New Orleans."[58]

Once Stewart's pamphlet became attached to the suspected uprising in Madison County, incidences of mob justice spread rapidly. Murderous rampages took place not only in Vicksburg, but also Natchez, Little Rock, New Orleans, Norfolk, Cincinnati, and as far east as Washington, DC.[59] While the racial component to the lynchings throughout Mississippi cannot be underestimated, it's important to note just how ostracized Vicksburg's community of white gamblers were. Like alcohol use and prostitution, gambling had long been associated with criminal and antireligious activity throughout American history. Temperance societies often linked alcohol consumption with other vices, and the veneer of sinfulness was strongly attached to gambling as one of the works of the devil.

Coupled with the fact that gambling involved myriad forms of deception if not outright theft, the institution was at once coveted by those seeking quick gain or amusement, while remaining a source of severe criticism and hostility. A month after the killings, the *Vicksburg Whig* ran a number of accounts of the lynchings originally printed in regional newspapers from Ohio to Alabama. The *Mobile Advertiser*'s sentiment is representative of these reflections:

> Of one fact we are satisfied—it is that the upright citizens of the several towns and villages along the whole Mississippi Valley, have been more often and more wantonly outraged by these gentleman "sportsmen," as they denominate themselves, than is conceived of, perhaps, in any other part of the civilized world. The arts that are used by them to win upon the confidence of their unsuspecting and innocent victims, and the wretchedness and ruin that follow upon the success of their stratagems, are calculated to excite, to the highest degree, not only the grief of the good and virtuous citizen, but to awaken the fire of his resentment, for the injuries and the degradation which are those inflicted upon society. These secret yet infamous marauders upon public private peace, it is believed are guilty of more heinous crimes than robbery and arson. There is little doubt if all hidden transactions were brought to light, there would be scenes of blood and horror disclosed, at which humanity would recoil and weep, and indignation burn![60]

In short, the gamblers deserved their fate. As Stewart recorded in the aftermath of the killings in Vicksburg, "Startling as [it] may seem to foreigners, it will ever reflect honour on the insulted citizens of Vicksburg, among those who best know how to appreciate the motives by which they were actuated. Their city now stands redeemed and ventilated from all the vices and influence of gambling and assignation houses [brothels]; two of the greatest curses that ever corrupted the morals of any community."[61]

Part of the warped but skillful genius of Virgil A. Stewart's conspiratorial account was his assigning responsibility for the suspected slave insurrection to Vicksburg's gamblers. By racializing their already unpopular trade, he was able to intensify the fears of whites against their presence in the city, while suggesting that whiteness alone was insufficient protective cover against Black vengeance. Stewart was tapping into a kind of racial McCarthyism—the suspicion of a fifth column among Southern white plantation owners. As a report justifying the killings one year later expressed it: "It was not believed that the execution of a few negroes, unknown and obscure, would have the effect of frightening their *white* associates from an attempt to perpetrate their horrid designs."[62]

As for the legendary John Murrell, the outlaw had no interest in liberating slaves. On the contrary, he was best known for "stealing" them and then reselling them—on occasion to the same owners, in a scheme known at the time as the "reverse underground railroad." Virgil A. Stewart was actually an informant who helped convict Murrell of thievery in early 1835 in Nashville, Tennessee. As historian Ben Wynne has written, Stewart used his newfound fame and clout among plantation owners as the man who brought Murrell to justice, to fabricate the story behind his incendiary pamphlet.

Using Stewart's word alone for a source, one Mississippi newspaper spread the alarm by warning its readers that "individuals enjoying all the privileges of free citizens, have, with fiend-like madness, instigated the ignorant and generally contented Africans to rise against their fellow citizens and to engage in in indiscriminate butchery of every age and sex."[63] With July 4 marked out as a day of terror, Stewart's pamphlet effectively began a countdown among slaveholders in the region, setting the stage for what would become a day of lynchings and shocking acts of violence throughout Vicksburg and its surrounding counties.

Outside of the South, within the intensifying abolitionist movement, the horrors of Vicksburg were seen in an entirely different light. The lynchings astonished a generation of antislavery thinkers and activists, as Vicksburg became synonymous with the terrorism associated with slavery. Five years later, the mob violence of Vicksburg still retained powerful emotional resonance. The 1840 publication of the *Anti-Slavery Almanac* featured the horrific violence at Vicksburg, depicting the lynching of the gamblers, but also the torture of Blacks and the assault (including one whipping) on innocent whites. The *Almanac* would prove to

Anti-Slavery Almanac *illustration: Vicksburg, 1840, "Our Peculiar Domestic Institutions," Library of Congress, Rare Book and Special Collections Division*

be a highly effective tool in countering the idea of an "idyllic" South, filled with happy slaves.

And it was an event powerful enough to pierce the fog of depression enveloping Abraham Lincoln and draw his attention. Indeed, despite the emotional toll life's turns were taking on him, the savagery of the Mississippi killings would make a lasting impression upon Lincoln for years to come.

WHILE LINCOLN'S FRIEND WILLIAM HERNDON WOULD LATER create a stir by suggesting that Ann Rutledge was the only woman Lincoln ever loved, there is little reason to doubt her death's effect upon his mental state. Decades later, Lincoln's New Salem friend John Hill would write that "Lincoln bore up under [her death] very well until some days afterward a heavy rain fell, which unnerved him—(and the balance you know)."[64] One of Ann's brothers would describe the overwrought Lincoln in great detail years later. "The effect upon Mr. Lincoln's mind was terrible," he wrote. "He had fits of great mental depression, and wandered up and down the river and into the woods woefully abstracted—at times in the deepest distress . . . we must admit he walked on that sharp and narrow line which divides sanity from insanity."[65]

Whether Ann's death was the catalyst of Lincoln's depression or a reflection of its underlying presence can never be fully known. Scholars continue to debate her death's effect on Lincoln.[66] Herman Melville, who knew the experience of depression well, perhaps put it best in his novel *Billy Budd*: "Who in the rainbow can draw the line where the violet tint ends and the orange tint begins? Distinctly we see the difference of the colors, but where exactly does the one first blendingly enter into the other? So with sanity and insanity."[67] Whatever the origin of his first major depression, it coincided with Rutledge's death, and it led friends to keep a watchful eye on him. "Lincoln told me that he felt like Committing Suicide often," Mentor Graham recalled.[68] While Lincoln had exhibited instances of melancholy

Earliest known photograph of Abraham Lincoln, 1846.
Nicholas H. Shepherd, 1846

before Rutledge's death, his deep depression now necessitated his friends' care that he didn't carry a knife.[69]

Lincoln stayed with his friend Bowling Green and his wife, Nancy, for two weeks after Rutledge's death.[70] Caring for the devastated Lincoln became a communal effort. Samuel Hill "had to lock him up and keep guard over him for some two weeks."[71] When longtime friend and political ally Isaac Cogdale had the heart to ask Lincoln, many years later, "Is it true that you ran a little wild about the matter?" referring to Rutledge, Lincoln acknowledged, "I did really—I run off the track. It was my first. I loved the woman dearly [and] sacredly."[72] Unsurprisingly, Lincoln neglected his duties as postmaster after Ann's death, burying himself in law books to the point of "momentary derangement," according to Mentor Graham.[73]

By December 1835, Lincoln had regained enough emotional fortitude to participate in a special session of the legislature held at Vandalia.[74] During this time, Lincoln championed the promotion of the Beardstown, Illinois, canal, among other public works projects. This is the period William Herndon suspected that Lincoln visited Beardstown. While there, Lincoln recounted that he had a "devilish passion" and contracted syphilis while seeing a prostitute. Herndon, mindful of protecting the now martyred president's reputation, was said to have regretted not having blotted out his note of the matter or "burned [it] to ashes."[75] While not impeaching Lincoln's fidelity to his wife, Mary Todd, Herndon stressed that "Lincoln was a man of terribly strong passions."[76]

As 1835 turned to 1836, Abraham Lincoln was a man weighted down by the encumbrances of a vanishing youth. He remained woefully in debt, unmarried, and romantically widowed; he lacked a steady profession and remained steeped in anguish and anxiety. The thought of taking his own life was ever-present. But these facts did not make up the entirety of Lincoln's standing in life. He was also a newly elected representative of a people who trusted and admired him. He had won friends willing to care for him in his miseries and misfortunes. And he had displayed a resilience to himself and others that warranted more respect than pity. Finally, in a season of great personal trial, Lincoln did not lose sight of the world of politics. His own district and state's needs were, of course, paramount. But he had taken note of far-off events—events that mattered to him and to the direction of the country. And he would not soon forget them.

TWO

1836: FAILING

Born in 1810 in Pittsburgh, one year after Abraham Lincoln, Francis McIntosh was a free Black man of mixed racial ancestry—a mulatto, in the language of the time.[1] And he was born one year before "the first steamboat ever floated on the Western rivers," as *The New York Times* described Livingston and Fulton's vessel's maiden voyage that traveled from Pittsburgh to New Orleans over fourteen days in 1811.[2] Described by a fellow crew member as "quiet and good natured," the twenty-six-year-old McIntosh was well accustomed to steamboat travel, serving as a cook and porter.[3]

The morning of McIntosh's murder began in Louisville, where a woman he'd recently fallen in love with—a chambermaid on another steamboat, the *Lady Jackson*—departed just ahead of him. The plan was to meet in St. Louis upon his arrival. With sunset scheduled just before seven o'clock, there would be a few hours of natural light left for McIntosh to display his new red jacket to the people of St. Louis, before meeting his companion.[4]

Like Vicksburg, some five hundred miles to its south, St. Louis was defined by its position along the Mississippi River.

Serving as a hub for steamboat travel, the city reflected a "new fluidity [that] characterized social relations and commerce, giving rise to new visions of social progress and perfection as well as to new fears of social disorder and decay."[5] Coupled with its "uneasy existence on the border of an increasingly distinct and antagonistic North and South," the city was shaped by novel forms of social and economic volatility.[6] By 1840, St. Louis's population had grown to nearly four times that of Chicago, with some 16,469 residents, giving it a ranking of twenty-fourth among America's largest cities.[7] All of this would change when St. Louis lost out to Chicago in the great westward railroad competition. But early on, St. Louis was the largest western city, enhancing its regional importance. When he left the *Flora* that Thursday afternoon, McIntosh was stepping into the most cosmopolitan city of the burgeoning American West.

Almost immediately after disembarking, he encountered trouble. First, two sailors ran past him. McIntosh didn't pay them much mind, but he next heard two officers call out to him to stop them. With no uniformed police in St. Louis at the time and two white men shouting at him, McIntosh didn't know what was happening.[8] When he failed to apprehend the fleeing sailors, Deputy Sheriff George Hammond and Deputy Constable William Mull arrested McIntosh instead.[9] He was then brought before the city's Justice Walsh, who promptly issued a "warrant for [his] commitment to jail."[10] At sundown, as he was being escorted out of court, McIntosh asked one of the officers, as they neared the courthouse square, what would be his punishment. Accounts vary as to what McIntosh was told, but as abolitionist accounts emphasized at the time, he had good reason to fear imprisonment in a slave state could mean losing not only his freedom, but perhaps his life as well.[11]

Upon hearing the response, McIntosh drew a knife and slashed at Mull, though he missed his mark. A subsequent strike caught Mull in the right side of the chest.[12] Hammond then grabbed McIntosh by the shoulder, eliciting a blow from McIntosh under the chin, creating a gaping wound. Dazed and bloodied, Hammond staggered about twenty paces before collapsing to his death.[13] McIntosh attempted to flee, but Mull called out for help, and McIntosh was soon surrounded. McIntosh was then taken to the jail on Sixth and Chestnut Streets, a growing crowd in pursuit.

Word spread fast about what had happened. St. Louis was hardly unfamiliar with violent crime at the time, including murder—but McIntosh's color and his killing of an officer made him an instant target for vengeance. Soon, the crowd, said to have included Hammond's wailing and grief-stricken widow and children, gathered outside the jail. Before long, a mob broke into McIntosh's cell and forcibly removed him. He was marched to Seventh and Chestnut Streets, near the outskirts of town. At this point, McIntosh was chained to an old locust tree, where members of the local fire company began stacking wood around his feet.[14] According to St. Louis's mayor at the time, who was part of the crowd, the mob took up the chant, "Burn him, burn him."[15] To their great satisfaction, McIntosh was then set on fire, as a thousand or more observed.[16]

William Lloyd Garrison's abolitionist newspaper, *The Liberator*, would provide a detailed account.

I have just returned from witnessing the most horrid sight that ever fell to the lot of man, viz: the execution of "Lynch Law" upon a yellow fellow, by the horrible means of a *slow fire*. The cause of this almost unprecedented execution, I will now briefly relate. Deputy Sheriff Hammond, while endeavoring to arrest the offender, was, by the above mentioned yellow fellow, defeated in his intent. During the scuffle, the prisoner escaped. Mr. Hammond then arrested the yellow fellow for his interference and took him before a Justice of the Peace, by whom he was committed. While conducting him to jail, accompanied by our constable, Mr. Mull, the prisoner, drew a knife and plunged it into the constable's side. Upon witnessing this, Hammond sprang at the prisoner, who now turned upon him and inflicted a terrible and mortal blow; the point of the knife struck him on the chin, passed through his throat, completely severing the jugular vein; he staggered a few paces and fell dead. The prisoner then fled to a yard or passage way, but being brought to bay by his pursuers, and still retaining his knife, he swore he would kill the first man who attempted to arrest him. His pursuers, perceiving his threatening manner, backed out with the exception of one, who seized the rail, broke it over his head, which slightly stunned him but soon recovering, he resumed his menacing attitude, when a powerful and courageous man, but just arrived, seized upon a stone and hurled it with herculean force, striking him on the shoulder and

St. Louis City Jail, Sixth Street and Chestnut Street, 1870

dislocating that limb. His arm dropped useless at his side, his knife fell from his grasp, and he was immediately arrested, bound, and carried to prison.

We must now return to the dead and wounded. During the time occupied in the pursuit of the prisoner, the news of the affray had spread over town, and the crowd around Mr. Hammond's body was joined by his son, (an interesting lad about 11 years of age, whose loud and heart-rending lamentations infuriated the already excited spectators). They swore that the murderer should not live another hour. This resolution once formed, they proceeded to the jail where the prisoner was confined. Being too strong for the officers, who could not, under existing circumstances, make much resistance, after forcing three doors they reached the cell that contained the murderer, and led him forth amidst the shouts of the multitude. Some endeavored to quell the tumult, but to no purpose. The friends of Mr. Hammond (and they were many, for he was universally beloved and respected) were determined on revenge—a revenge that may seem to you unwarrantable, but take the case home to yourself, conceive your own brother in the situation of Mr. Hammond, and you will find some palliating considerations to abate the horrid character of this transaction.

The mob conducted the murderer to a pasture back of the city with the intention of hanging him, but some among them cried out, "Burn him." The horrible suggestion was immediately caught at; the moon had now risen bright and clear—the evening was calm and beautiful—too fair a night for the appalling spectacle that was to be witnessed by at least five hundred of our most respectable citizens. They chained the murderer to a tree, and the cry arose, "Let the fire be slow!" They piled shavings and rails around him until they reached the height of about 2½ feet—a match was applied to the shavings—and the murderer commenced singing a hymn, which he continued until the heat became intense, and then these few half-smothered words escaped him, "God take my life!"

I had pressed forward until I stood in front of the sufferer—I could not move—it seemed as though some horrid fascination chained me to the spot, and I witnessed all his agony. Never [a] martyr suffered more courageously. Not one single scream escaped him—his chest heaved with the most intense agony, yet all he said was "God take my soul!—God take my life!" in accents so low that none except those immediately about him could catch the sound. He had been burning about fifteen minutes, when someone said, "He feels no pain, he is too far gone"; he immediately answered, "Y-e-s, I d-o f-e-e-l i-t!" Never, never can I forget his looks when with the utmost difficulty he uttered those few words. The fire was so low that his legs and feet were burnt to almost to a cinder before his other parts were to any degree affected. The tree to which he was chained was in full blossom, and he seemed to smile upon the horrid deed. The horror of the scene can never be effaced from my memory! Imagine a human being chained to a tree—a slow fire burning around him—the boiling blood gushing in torrents from his mouth—his legs burnt to a crisp—yet his head moving from side to side, and occasionally a half uttered groan. But I will not, I cannot, further enlarge upon so horrible—I feel a sickness at my heart, a dizziness in my head, occasioned by witnessing this terrific sight; but I was rooted to the spot, I could not withdraw my eye from the sight before me. M.C.[17]

Burning of McIntosh at St. Louis, in April, 1836.

"Burning of McIntosh at St. Louis," illustration from the American Anti-Slavery Almanac.

Six years after McIntosh's murder, Charles Dickens wrote a letter to his biographer, John Forster, during his visit to St. Louis, recounting the episode. "It is not six years ago," Dickens wrote, "since a slave in this very same St. Louis, being arrested (I forgot for what), and knowing he had no chance of a fair trial, be his offense what it might, drew his bowie knife and ripped the constable across the body. A scuffle ensuing, the desperate negro stabbed two others with the same weapon. The mob who gathered round (among whom were men of mark, wealth, and influence in the place) overpowered him by numbers, carried him away to a piece of open ground beyond the city; *and burned him alive.*"[18] Dickens got a number of facts wrong, including the assumption that McIntosh was a slave. But Dickens's account underscored the enormous attention McIntosh's killing continued to draw, even years later. Yet, despite his revulsion at the atrocity, like so many who would recount the incident, Dickens failed to mention McIntosh by name.

One man, a young former Princeton theology student turned editor, would visit the site of McIntosh's death the next day.

A ghoulish retrieval of "mementos" from the tree that was to take place over the years was already underway.[19] The editor's name was Elijah, and McIntosh's death would affect him, and the future of the antislavery movement, powerfully in the years to come. After seeing the remains of McIntosh on April 29, Elijah P. Lovejoy, choked with grief, would write that what he and others witnessed was so profound, that "out of bitterness of heart, [we] prayed that [we] might not live."[20]

THE KILLING OF MCINTOSH HAS BEEN DESCRIBED AS "arguably the first lynching in the history of the United States."[21] McIntosh's murder set in motion a series of influential events, beginning with the fateful condemnation of his killing by radical white abolitionist Elijah P. Lovejoy. Lovejoy would himself be murdered the following year by a mob, his death making up the final act in a trio of mob killings that began in Mississippi, that Abraham Lincoln would memorialize in his Lyceum Address.

If McIntosh was turned into a kind of martyr by abolitionists in later years, it was a counter to his early demonization, beginning with the invective heaped upon him by the aptly named Judge Luke E. Lawless, who, on May 16, presided over the grand jury in the aftermath of McIntosh's lynching. A "prejudicial" pro-slavery Democrat described by St. Louis lawyers as "imperious, overbearing, and disrespectful," Lawless was to decide whether or not charges should be brought against anyone for McIntosh's death.[22] Lawless told the grand jury that McIntosh's demeanor was "atrocious and savage," warning that "the free negro has been converted into a deadly enemy."[23] It was a sentiment in keeping with Alexis de Tocqueville's prediction of what freedom might portend for African Americans, a year before McIntosh's killing. "If one absolutely had to foresee the future," Tocqueville predicted, "I would say that, following the probable course of things, the abolition of slavery in the South will increase the repugnance for blacks felt by the white population."[24] Lawless's belief underscored Tocqueville's prediction that Black freedom would evoke greater fears than Blacks in captivity.

McIntosh's free status, along with his biracial background, represented a basic affront to white supremacy and the racial hierarchy it sought to protect. That *The Liberator*'s eyewitness account described McIntosh as a "yellow fellow" three times in the opening paragraph conveys the novelty and unease experienced by Blacks of multiracial ancestry, caught between two worlds. Racial amalgamation and the presumed wantonness in character freedom was thought to establish in Blacks threatened political order and stability throughout the United States, but perhaps more so in states like Missouri, where slavery and Black freedom readily intermingled.

In the end, Lawless argued, Blacks possessed "a fiery unreasoning instinct . . . uniformly marked by ruthless, remorseless revenge."[25] Lawless instructed the grand jury that no one could rightly be charged, as the complications of so many acting in unison would not allow for responsibility to be properly assigned. While the nature of McIntosh's murder violated the Constitution's prohibition against cruel and unusual punishment, his killing of Hammond afflicted the crowd of whites by a "mysterious, metaphysical, and almost electric phrenzy," Lawless argued. "The case then transcends your jurisdiction—it is beyond the reach of human law."[26] In one fell swoop, Lawless had made lynching a near spiritual right.

That McIntosh and his tragic story is not better known is perhaps unsurprising, given how endemic the purposeful forgetting of racial violence afflicted against African Americans and other racial minorities has been throughout American history. And yet, many Americans know that John Brown's 1859 raid at Harpers Ferry in Virginia was, in many respects, one of the catalyzing events leading to the Civil War. Brown's radical abolitionism was at least in part inspired by the murder of Elijah P. Lovejoy, whose own death was, in part, the result of his condemnations of McIntosh's lynching. As Lovejoy biographer David S. Reynolds notes, Brown pledged his antipathy toward slavery at a prayer meeting where he learned of Lovejoy's murder from a theology professor from Western Reserve College. "Here, before God, in the presence of these witnesses, from this time, I consecrate my life to the destruction of slavery!" Brown pledged, standing before the congregation.[27] The McIntosh-Lovejoy-Brown connection is one of the more insightful but less-explored threads leading to the American Civil War.

In the ensuing years, white women abolitionists tended to see McIntosh's death as evidence of his martyrdom, while white male abolitionists tended to view his death as a prelude to Lovejoy's. Either way, McIntosh became a symbol of slavery's depravity—his free status notwithstanding.[28] Today, members of the St. Louis community have worked to keep the memory of Francis McIntosh alive. On April 30, 2021, 185 years after his death, members of the Reparative Justice Coalition of St. Louis gathered in Kiener Plaza to remember the life and death of Francis McIntosh in a small soil gathering ceremony near the site of his murder.[29] The following year, students, staff, and faculty of Washington University in St. Louis participated in the commemoration, as one of its prominent trustees and "major benefactor[s] John O'Fallon is said to have served as foreman of the grand jury that declined to bring an indictment against perpetrators of [McIntosh's] lynching, as advised by the presiding Judge Luke E. Lawless. One of WashU's early buildings, O'Fallon Polytechnic Institute, opened in 1867 at 7th and Chestnut, the very intersection where Francis McIntosh was burned alive by a mob three decades earlier. Ironically, WashU School of Law began in that building, at this historic St. Louis intersection marred by corruption of the rule of law."[30] To this day, there remains no public memorial to Francis McIntosh in St. Louis.

DESPITE THE TENOR OF HIS TIMES, ABRAHAM LINCOLN proved to be far less inclined than his contemporaries to draw racist assumptions about the innate characteristics of Blacks. Some of this had to do with his antipathy toward slavery, while other aspects of his views were likely occasioned by his own experiences. Some have mused that Lincoln's revulsion toward slavery began during his childhood, when his father, Thomas Lincoln, hired him out to work his farm and those of his neighbors to pay off his growing debts. This form of quasi-slavery, as Lincoln biographer Michael Burlingame describes it, was an indelible early life experience for Lincoln. From around his sixteenth birthday "Lincoln was virtually a slave, toiling as a butcher, ferry operator, riverman, store clerk, farmhand, wood chopper, distiller, and sawyer, earning anywhere from 10 cents to 31 cents a day. He handed these meager wages over to [his father] Thomas in compliance with the law stipulating that children were the property of their father and that any money they earned belonged to him. Locked in this bondage, Abraham felt as if he were chattel on a Southern plantation. 'I used to be a slave,' [Lincoln] declared in 1856. This painful experience led him to identify with the slaves and to denounce human bondage even when it was politically risky to do so."[31]

Suffice it to say, this form of labor was hardly tantamount to racial slavery. Nevertheless, Lincoln's views reflected an antebellum antipathy toward exploitative labor. When Herman Melville had Ishmael, his protagonist in *Moby-Dick* (1851), declare, "Who ain't a slave?" he was affirming a bond with enslaved African Americans and exploited white laborers.[32] As historian Eric Foner has written, "many Americans experienced the expansion of capitalism not as an enhancement of the power to shape their world, but as a loss of control over their own lives. . . . The metaphor that crystallized this discontent—'wage slavery'—implicitly challenged the contrast between free and slave labor."[33]

It's most likely that Lincoln first experienced the horrors of slavery in 1828 and 1831, when, as a flatboatman, he visited New Orleans and saw the evils of the institution up close. Lincoln reportedly told his friend Allen Gentry, who accompanied him to New Orleans in 1828, "Allen, that's a disgrace," after Lincoln witnessed a girl being examined on the auction block. Other Lincoln biographers remain skeptical.[34] Likewise, Lincoln's cousin John Hanks would claim, "I Can say knowingly that it was on this trip that [Lincoln] formed his opinions of Slavery: it ran its iron in him then & there."[35]

Can we be sure that New Orleans "was the first time, but not the last time, that [Lincoln] would be repelled while observing slavery firsthand?"[36] Maybe not. But what may be more significant, and less debated, is that Lincoln and his crew were robbed by a group of enslaved Blacks from a nearby plantation on one of their trips to New Orleans. As Henry Louis Gates Jr. notes, "the incidents strongly suggest how Lincoln could have developed such deep animosity for the institution of slavery side by side with such unbending belief in the necessity of racial segregation."[37] Instead, Lincoln attached no racially based significance to the episode.

Another example—one in Lincoln's own hand—demonstrating his disdain for slavery, can be found in an 1841 letter to his friend Joshua Speed's half-sister, Mary. In it, Lincoln recounts a visit to St. Louis, where McIntosh had been lynched five years earlier, noting how the enslaved bore the horrors of the institution with great resilience.

> A gentleman had purchased twelve negroes in different parts of Kentucky and was taking them to a farm in the South. They were chained six and six together. A small iron clevis was around the left wrist of each, and this fastened to the main chain by a shorter one at a convenient distance from the others; so that the negroes were strung together precisely like so many fish upon a trot-line. In this condition they were being separated forever from the scenes of their childhood, their friends, their fathers and mothers, and brothers and sisters, and many of them, from their wives and children, and going into perpetual slavery where the lash of the master is proverbially more ruthless and unrelenting than any other where; and yet amid all these distressing circumstances, as we would think them, they were the most cheerful and apparantly [*sic*] happy creatures on board.[38]

On the one hand, Lincoln's letter to Mary Speed might be confused with the tired trope of the "happy slave." Yet, Lincoln's emphasis on the "ruthless" and "unrelenting" lash of the master, is integral to understanding that Black joy in the face of slavery's horrors was not in service of an institution they were satisfied in—as South Carolina's John C. Calhoun and other Southern politicians would argue—but rather one in which they had learned to retain their humanity against all odds.

That said, Lincoln's personal and political opposition to slavery was held along with the folk racism and politics of white supremacy familiar to the time and region of the country he grew up in. The inconsistencies have led any number of historians and critics of Lincoln to argue one side or the other: that he was virulently antiracist and antislavery altogether, or he was hypocrisy personified—a mere servant of political whim. Yet, unlike Thomas Jefferson, whose Declaration of Independence Lincoln would revere, Lincoln invited considerable political risk in his career over the subject of slavery—and Francis McIntosh's story would be a part of it.

The spring and summer of 1836 were busy seasons for Lincoln. He was deeply engaged in his legal studies, hoping to finally become a practicing lawyer. And he was in the midst of preparing for his reelection campaign. Unbeknownst to him at the time, another romantic imbroglio was on the horizon. For now, the gruesome tale of Francis McIntosh would have to wait for the right moment for Lincoln to say what he needed to say on this second, and latest, example of mob violence and murder on the Mississippi River.

FOUR WEEKS AFTER THE GRAND JURY MET AND ABSOLVED the mob of any guilt in the murder of McIntosh, the *Sangamo Journal* published Abraham Lincoln's declaration of candidacy. "In your paper of last Saturday," Lincoln wrote, "I see a communication over the signature of 'Many Voters,' in which the candidates who are announced in the *Journal*, are called upon to 'show their hands.' Agreed. Here's mine!"[39] The cheeky announcement contained some hints of Lincoln's political considerations in 1836. While opposed to slavery, he carved out a position equally opposed to Black voting rights—while somewhat playfully supportive of women's suffrage. "I go for all sharing the privileges of the government," Lincoln continued, "who assist in bearing its burthens. Consequently, I go for admitting all whites to the right of suffrage, who pay taxes or bear arms (by no means excluding females)."[40] He closed out the short statement by expressing his desire to "dig canals and construct rail roads, without borrowing money and paying interest in it." Lincoln's last sentence began with a bit of black humor. "If alive on the first Monday in November," Lincoln wrote, "I shall vote for [the Whig presidential candidate] Hugh L. White for President."[41]

Lincoln would be alive the first Monday in November, finishing first on August 1, in a field of sixteen candidates. The campaign was a grueling one, with Lincoln traveling by horseback from one small town to another, getting into the occasional verbal scrap with his opponents, as national politics—it was a presidential election year after all—crept into the local issues of the day.[42] Lincoln acquitted himself well in his reelection bid, demonstrating remarkable speaking skills at times. As Joshua Speed recalled, Lincoln masterfully took down an opponent named George Forquer, who had left the Whig party to become a Democrat.

Forquer had recently erected a lightning rod on the roof of his house—a novelty Lincoln, like many at the time, had not seen. The rod became fodder for Lincoln's acerbic political wit. "The gentleman [Forquer] has seen fit to allude to my being a young man; but he forgets that I am older in years than I am in the tricks and trades of politicians," Lincoln said. "I desire to live, and I desire place and distinction; but I would rather die now than, like the gentleman, live to see the day that I would change my politics for an office worth three thousand dollars a year, and then feel compelled to erect a lightning rod to protect a guilty conscience from an offended God."[43] With his wit and political talents becoming ever more apparent, Lincoln would become the Whig floor leader in the General Assembly, as a member of the so-called "Long Nine"—nine Sangamo County legislators known for their height. He was also named chairman of the finance committee, despite being a member of the minority party.[44]

After his reelection in August, Lincoln was finally licensed to practice law on September 9, 1836. His intense study of the law had helped to restore Lincoln's "equilibrium" in the months after Ann Rutledge's death.[45] Pursuing his studies with uncommon doggedness and long periods of isolation that often traversed into the antisocial, Lincoln had found his profession. The "twenty-four hour periods without food or sleep . . . often walking unconscious, his head on one side, thinking and talking to himself," had paid off.[46]

If Lincoln's melancholy "dripped from him as he walked," as William Herndon would describe it, he now had a full-time profession to at least abate, if not remove, his flood of sorrowful emotions.[47] Managing depression would become a lifelong struggle for Lincoln. This first sharp bout after Rutledge's death could not be well hidden from his colleagues. As Robert L. Wilson, who ran as a fellow candidate with Lincoln in the 1836 election recalled, Lincoln once shared with him "that although he appeared to enjoy life rapturously, Still he was the victim of terrible melancholy. He Sought company, and indulged in fun and hilarity without restraint, or Stint as to time. Still when by himself, he told me that he was so overcome with mental depression, that he never dare carry a knife in his pocket. And as long as I was intimately acquainted with him, previous to his commencement of the law, he never carried a pocket knife."[48] In late 1836, Lincoln would find himself caught up in a new and fleeting romantic entanglement that would add to his anguish.

"Mr. L had a double consciousness, a double life," William Herndon would recall. "In one moment he was in a state of abstraction and then quickly in another state when he was social, talkative, and a communicative fellow."[49] This double life of Lincoln's took center stage in 1836, when, still reeling from debt, depression, and grief, he was engaged in a bizarre courtship sometime in the fall with Mary Owens, a twenty-eight-year-old Kentucky society woman he had met briefly in October of 1833 during a visit to her sister. L. M. "Nult" Greene, who became part of Owens's family through marriage, described her as "*tall* & portly weighed in 1836 about 180 lbs at this time she was 29 or 30 years of age—had large blue eyes with the finest trimmings I ever saw. She was jovial social loved wit & humor—had a liberal English education & was considered wealthy."[50]

The bizarre quality of their prospective marriage had to do with Lincoln's having seemingly promised to Mary's sister, Elizabeth, that "if Mary Owens ever came back to New Salem, he would marry her."[51] Today, we'd call Lincoln's dalliance with Mary Owens a classic "rebound" relationship—and Lincoln clearly regretted it. Initially, Lincoln "thought her intelligent and agreeable, and saw no good objection to plodding through life hand in hand with her."[52] But Lincoln soon soured on the prospect upon Mary's return. "I knew she was over-size," he

Mary Owens

said, "but now she now appeared a fair match for Falstaff."[53] The strange courtship revealed elements of Lincoln's double consciousness, Herndon observed. Here was Lincoln, again, now newly reelected, without romantic prospects or money, hurling himself into an economically stable and socially affirming role as would-be groom—all the while romantically uninterested.

Lincoln's letters to Owens reveal this inner turmoil and a kind of desperation to get himself out of one kind of failure (remaining single beyond what was socially acceptable) in exchange for another (dishonorably breaking off a marriage proposal). This moment in Lincoln's life has been described as one marked by "[p]overty, ignominy, failure, and unhappiness."[54] Now, facing a marriage he felt obligated to commence but didn't want, he was damned if he did and damned if he didn't. In a letter to Mary the following spring, Lincoln presented her with the proverbial "it's not you, it's me" offer of a relationship.

> Whatever woman may cast her lot with mine should any ever do so, it is my intention to do all in my power to make her happy and contented; and there is nothing I can imagine, that would make me now unhappy than to fail in the effort. I know I should be much happier with you than the way I am, provided I saw no signs of discontent in you. What you have said to me may have been in jest, or I may have misunderstood it. If so, then let it be forgotten; if otherwise, I much wish you would think seriously before you decide. For my part I have already decided. What I have said I will most positively abide by, provided you wish it. My opinion is that you had better not do it. You have not been accustomed to hardship, and it may be more severe than you now imagine. I know you are capable of thinking correctly on any subject, and if you deliberate maturely upon this, before you decide, then I am willing to abide your decision.[55]

"You better not do it" is hardly an enticing invitation to marriage, and Owens saw it for what it was. But in the interim period, while the possibility hung in the balance, Lincoln was unable to escape the throes of his first great bout of depression, the one that began at the time of Ann Rutledge's death.

• • •

LINCOLN'S POWERFUL EPISODES OF DEPRESSION CAN BE broken into "period[s] of intense work . . . profound personal stress . . . and bleak weather."[56] All three were present in 1836—this, despite Lincoln's political successes. A scene from the close of that year's legislative session speaks volumes. As Lincoln returned from the capital of Vandalia in March 1837 with three other legislators who were sharing a room together, his friend and colleague William Butler recounted his experience with Lincoln's fragile emotional state:

> I was at Vandalia the last winter he spent there. Lincoln, myself, and two others travelled home together on horseback, after the fashion of those times. We stopped over night here at Henderson's Point, and all slept on the floor, We were tired, and the rest slept pretty well. But I noticed from the first that Lincoln was uneasy, turning over and thinking, and studying, so much so that he kept me awake.
>
> At last, I said to him, "Lincoln what is the matter with you?"
>
> "Well" said he "I will tell you. All the rest of you have something to look forward to, and all are glad to get home, and will have something to do when you get there. But it isn't so with me. I am going home, Butler, without a thing in the world. I have drawn all my pay I got at Vandalia, and have spent it all. I am in debt—I am owing to Van Bergen, and he has levied on my horse and my compass, and I have nothing to pay the debt with, and no way to make any money. I don't know what to do.[57]

Beyond his financial hardships, Lincoln was also still wrestling with how to get out of his relationship with Mary Owens. Having lost a love interest he desired, only to become entangled with one he did not, Lincoln, at twenty-seven, had ample reason to lament his station in life. Given his overall state of affairs, it's fair to say that the world of politics—and the care of his friends—was all Lincoln had going for him at the close of 1836.

The political world was beset with its own trials as the murder of Francis McIntosh had so grimly revealed. The gruesome mob violence in Vicksburg, Mississippi, was now working its way up, as it were, to St. Louis—one state removed from Lincoln's Illinois. Where Vicksburg was a world away—some six hundred miles south, St. Louis was a mere one hundred miles from Springfield. Growing anxiety about the creeping mob violence and the future of American democracy became part of local political discourse. "Do the signs of the present times indicate the downfall of the government?" was presented as a subject for a lecture in Springfield, in late 1836.[58] It was a concern of deep importance to Lincoln, but he was not yet prepared to add his voice to the discussion. It would take another year, and another episode of mob violence, this time in his home state of Illinois, to draw Lincoln, however temporarily, out of his personal darkness to say something about the darkness enveloping America.

➝ THREE ➝

1837: SEARCHING

When he was running for president in 1860, Abraham Lincoln was asked by John L. Scripps of the *Chicago Press & Tribune* if he could publish Lincoln's campaign autobiography. Lincoln agreed, hoping to produce something of value to the Republican Party in introducing him to the nation. Scripps's June interview of Lincoln in Springfield produced a thirty-two-page pamphlet, published in the *New York Tribune* in mid-July.[1] In it, Lincoln, writing in the third person, recalled his first public statement against slavery with great detail, citing the page numbers of the *Illinois House Journal* twenty-three years earlier, where his protest was registered. "In the autumn of 1836, he obtained a law license, and on April 15, 1837, removed to Springfield, and commenced the practice—his old friend Stuart taking him into partnership," Lincoln wrote. Then Lincoln recalled, "March 3, 1837, by a protest entered upon the *Illinois House Journal* of that date, at pages 817 and 818, Abraham, with Dan Stone, another representative of Sangamon, briefly defined his position on the slavery question; and so far as it goes, it was the same then as now."[2]

The specificity with which Lincoln recalled the statement speaks volumes about its significance to his career. Lincoln's early political positions were those of a centrist Whig, in a centrist state, with a conservative electorate on the slavery question. His modulated opposition to Andrew Jackson and support for internal improvements were one thing. The slavery question, however, posed a host of challenges. Congress had, just the year before, tabled all discussion on slavery by imposing a "gag order," underscoring the implacability of the issue. And in January of 1837, the Illinois legislature passed a resolution at once lamenting "the unfortunate condition of our fellow men, whose lots are cast in thraldom in a land of liberty and peace," while at the same time declaring "the right of property in slaves, is sacred to the slave-holding States by the Federal Constitution, and that they cannot be deprived of that right without their consent."[3]

The easiest thing for Lincoln to do would have been to do nothing. The measure declaring slavery a "sacred right" had passed by a 77–6 vote in the House and 18–0 in the Senate.[4] Putting it differently, of the other one hundred Illinois representatives voting on the measure with Lincoln, only five were opposed. Illinois had become a battleground for the slavery question with the American Anti-Slavery Society's mailing of abolitionist pamphlets to Southern states generating fierce opposition in the South against Northern states' interference with their "way of life."[5] As the January resolution put it, "We highly disapprove of the formation of abolition societies, and of the doctrines promulgated by them."[6]

The small but growing influx of abolitionists into northern Illinois from New England had generated strong antipathies toward the antislavery cause.[7] In many ways, America's long history of the vilification of "outside agitators" began in the 1830s with the rise of abolitionist societies. Indeed, when scouring about to find someone, anyone, to sign on to a statement in opposition to slavery, Lincoln could only find Dan Stone, "a native of Vermont and a graduate of Middlebury College who was not seeking reelection."[8] Nevertheless, in March of 1837, Lincoln decided to side with 5 percent of lawmakers in his state, and to raise his voice as the only politician interested in holding elective office in Illinois to publicly declare his opposition to slavery.

And Illinois was hardly trending toward a more progressive future with respect to race. A decade later in 1848, Illinois voters would approve a change to the state's constitution banning the further emigration of African Americans into the state, a measure that went into effect in 1853.[9] Why, then, did Lincoln voice his opposition to slavery at this time? Looking at Lincoln and Stone's resolution, we can see that it was not without regard to political self-interest or recognition of the broad white opposition in the state toward abolition:

> Protest in Illinois Legislature on Slavery
> March 3, 1837
>
> The following protest was presented to the House, which was read and ordered to be spread on the journals, to wit:
>
> "Resolutions upon the subject of domestic slavery having passed both branches of the General Assembly at its present session, the undersigned hereby protest against the passage of the same.
>
> They believe that the institution of slavery is founded on both injustice and bad policy; but that the

> promulgation of abolition doctrines tends rather to increase than to abate its evils.
>
> They believe that the Congress of the United States has no power, under the Constitution, to interfere with the institution of slavery in the different States.
>
> They believe that the Congress of the United States has the power, under the Constitution, to abolish slavery in the District of Columbia; but that that power ought not to be exercised unless at the request of people of said District.
>
> The difference between these opinions and those contained in the said resolutions, is their reason for entering this protest."
>
> Dan Stone,
> A. Lincoln,
> Representatives from the county of Sangamon

Historians are nearly universal in agreement: Lincoln had nothing to gain by publicly condemning slavery, varyingly describing the March 1837 resolution as a "politically courageous act," a "remarkably bold gesture," a "display of genuine political courage," and, finally, "not [to] be underestimated."[10] One Lincoln biographer, Douglas L. Wilson, sees Lincoln's decision as mysterious—not an effort to put Lincoln on the record as a "lonely [voice] crying out in the wilderness against the evils of slavery," but rather "something else, even though, unfortunately, it is not possible to say with precision what that something else was."[11]

After wading into the waters of these many takes on the subject, I've concluded the most obvious reason for Lincoln's public stance against slavery was that he simply abhorred it. This, of course, didn't mean Lincoln was unmindful of the political calculations needed in expressing his position. He couched his description of slavery as a form of "injustice and bad policy"—one that produces "evils"—while castigating abolitionists for their "promulgation" of doctrines that added to the evil. This was more a criticism of form than substance, but it left Lincoln on the side of the vast majority of his colleagues and the electorate. Additionally, Lincoln voiced legitimate constitutional concerns; concerns that would weigh upon him until the issuing of the Emancipation Proclamation—namely, how to preserve the dictates of the law while removing a fundamentally immoral institution.

By March of 1837, Lincoln had shared in writing his unambiguous desire to uphold the two core (but frequently conflicting) principles that would define his life's work: human freedom and the rule of law. His position was that of a minority of one, so he sifted among the few dissenting antislavery lawmakers to get at least one other cosigner for the statement condemning slavery—a requirement to print any protest in the Illinois House. As the only elected official in the state facing reelection to publicly declare slavery an evil and an injustice, it's fair to assume that Lincoln was acting out of conscience. Whether the outbursts of mob violence in Vicksburg or St. Louis had in any way contributed to Lincoln's stance against slavery is hard to know. But it was during this period that he so uniquely and categorically expressed it. "I am naturally anti-slavery," Lincoln would say, decades later. "If slavery is not wrong, nothing is wrong. I can not remember when I did not so think, and feel."[12] It was during this formative period in Lincoln's life that those feelings were translating for the first time into action. In the end, with his political career before him, and with much to lose should he choose differently, Lincoln sided with human freedom.

THE TRAGIC STORY OF ELIJAH P. LOVEJOY MAKES UP THE third in the series of murders that became essential components of Abraham Lincoln's first major political speech. That Lovejoy's murder at the hands of proslavery whites occurred in Lincoln's state of Illinois made for powerful crosswinds of opinion that Lincoln would have to address. Who was Elijah P. Lovejoy and how did this New England preacher-turned-publisher incite a national upheaval? How did he come to play such an important role in shaping the core beliefs and arguments Lincoln would make concerning slavery and the rule of law?

At the time of Lincoln's reelection in August of 1836, there appeared a curious article in the *Sangamo Journal*. The story was about a "Mr. Lovejoy, of *The Observer*" who "sent his printing apparatus to Alton, with the design of continuing his paper there." The *St. Louis Observer* started out as a mildly antislavery newspaper across the river from Alton, Illinois, with Elijah P. Lovejoy as its editor. In time, *The Observer* became a fiercely abolitionist paper, and Lovejoy, a marked man in slaveholding Missouri. The people of Alton only agreed to take Lovejoy and his press in, the article noted, because "having pledged himself, should [Lovejoy] continue his paper there, to cease defending abolition principles."[13] Lovejoy would break this promise, and in doing so, usher in a national firestorm over slavery and abolition.

Elijah Parish Lovejoy was born in the small town of Albion, Maine, on November 9, 1802, to the congregationalist minister Rev. Daniel Lovejoy and Elizabeth Pattee Lovejoy, a widely read and intellectually grounded woman.[14] Elijah was the oldest of nine children in this deeply religious family. Graduating from Waterville College—what would later become Colby College—Lovejoy decided to move west after a short stint teaching in Maine.[15] After taking upon himself the extraordinary challenge of walking to Boston from Maine, Lovejoy eventually found his way to St. Louis, arriving in 1827 by more conventional means.[16] An inveterate "wanderer" at the time, in his own words, he decided to found a school in what was the fastest growing city in the American West.[17]

In 1830, Lovejoy's restlessness would lead him to sell his school and become a co-owner and publisher of the *St. Louis Times*. It was in his role as editor at the *Times* where Lovejoy's New England religious values took on political significance. The *Times* was a strong supporter of Henry Clay—and feverishly opposed to the presidency of Andrew Jackson. "With an adulterer and murderer for our President, and fools and knaves for

Elijah P. Lovejoy

his advisers," Lovejoy would write of Jackson, "if we survive, than [*sic*] shall I believe that Providence intends to perpetuate our existence."[18] Despite his harsh view of Jackson, as Lovejoy biographer Ken Ellingwood has written, "slavery and its foes appeared to be of no concern to the St. Louis editor." Indeed, "Lovejoy's *Times* served to promote the trade in slaves by advertising auctions or serving as a go-between in posted notices that offered slaves without naming the seller."[19]

Lovejoy's restless spirit would again resurface in 1832, when, lacking the sort of passionate religious fervor he saw others experiencing at the First Presbyterian Church he had been attending in St. Louis, he decided to attend Princeton's Theological Seminary in March, with the hopes of joining the clergy.[20] The Princeton experience proved transformative. Lovejoy attained the religious devotion he had been lacking, although it did not produce the fervent abolitionism with which he would later be identified. Now an ordained minister, Lovejoy decided to pursue his new calling back in St. Louis, rather than in Maine, where the prospect of leading a congregation was the next logical step. Writing to his brother Owen in August of 1833, Lovejoy wrote:

> I wish it that it was in my power, consistently with duty, to come down and see "home" once more, but I think the indications of Providence are such as forbid it. They are impatiently calling me to the West, and to the West I must go.[21]

Back in St. Louis, Lovejoy would be enticed by fellow Presbyterians to start a newspaper with a religious mission.[22] The *St. Louis Observer* would be the result, beginning with its first issue in November of 1833. *The Observer* would not immediately become a bastion of radical abolitionist opinion, however. Lovejoy had been exposed to a variety of theological opinions about slavery while at Princeton, including abolitionism. As Ellingwood has noted, "At first, Lovejoy tiptoed into the slavery issue. His Princeton training had left him a committed gradualist, convinced that it was up to slave owners to choose the time and method for stepping onto the righteous path of emancipation. It was his job as minister and editor to preach, write, and publish in order to help them come to this righteous conclusion."[23] Like Lincoln at the time, Lovejoy was very much a moderate on the question of abolition, adopting colonization as the best solution to slavery, in contrast to abolitionists such as William Lloyd Garrison, whose *Liberator* newspaper, founded in 1831, called for immediate emancipation.

With this cautious approach as his first public foray into the slavery question, Lovejoy was nevertheless engaged with the issue, and his spiritual yearnings would serve to further radicalize him before long. His first public statement against slavery in the *St. Louis Observer* staked out a middle position—chiding "some of our Abolitionist brethren"—who thought moderates on the issue lacked courage, while at the same time seeing slavery as "a curse, politically and morally to every state where it exits."[24] In language that would resemble Lincoln's, Lovejoy argued, "Certain it is, that in this controversy, no one will be persuaded by naked denunciation or misrepresentations—but cool and temperate argument supported by facts, must perform the work."[25]

Nevertheless, in a cryptic ending to his statement in *The Observer*, Lovejoy suggested he might well be willing to change his mind.

> But we will not extend our remarks. Our object is peace and concert in action with every good man, in every good work. We are not sensible that we possess any prejudices upon the subject. We do not promise by any means, that we shall not become an Abolitionist, strictly, at some future day . . . but arguments of sufficient weight must be laid before us in order to this consummation.[26]

Was Lovejoy already sensing the pull to adopt the abolitionist position of immediate emancipation in 1834? It would seem so. By the end of 1835, *The Observer* "regularly carried items about slavery, many of them from the exchange papers that came in sacks of mail from the East Coast, where the growing abolitionist movement was now making liberal use of the printing press to spread its calls for emancipation."[27] Matters grew to a head when on October 1, 1835, Lovejoy "published the full declaration of principles of the American Anti-Slavery Society."[28] He was making good on the seed planted in his maiden article on slavery in *The Observer*.

It was a dangerous move, as vocal antislavery whites frequently became the targets of proslavery forces. Lovejoy's transformation invited the risk of physical violence, including death. In 1835, two whites who had assisted in the transportation of a group of slaves from Missouri to Illinois across the Mississippi River were summarily whipped a total of two hundred times upon discovery by sixty townspeople, before confessing. While their lives were spared, the message was as clear in Missouri as it had been in Mississippi: Any whites who supported the liberation of enslaved Blacks were risking their own lives. Lovejoy was well aware of the risk he was taking. "I am accused of being an Abolitionist," he wrote to his brother Owen on November 2, 1835, "and threatened in the newspapers of the city, and throughout the city, as well as various places in the state, with violence. *I expect it.* I expect that I shall be Lynched, or tarred and feathered, or it may be, hung up."[29] As prepared as Lovejoy may have been in the fall of 1835, his safety would become more precarious in the coming months. The murder of Francis McIntosh six months later would prove to be the harbinger of not only Lovejoy's last days in St. Louis, but, tragically, his last days alive.

LOVEJOY HAD ALREADY BEEN WEIGHING A MOVE TO ALTON, Illinois, by late 1835. He had visited the city before deciding to move there permanently, coming to see it as a potential sanctuary from the dangers lurking about him in St. Louis.[30] But the horrific killing of Francis McIntosh unleashed a series of events that forced his hand. Lovejoy was anguished by the murder, visiting the site of the burning the following day.[31] In his May 5, 1836, column condemning McIntosh's murder, Lovejoy was careful not to indict all of St. Louis for the barbarism he described in great detail.

> We have drawn the above gloomy and hideous picture, not for the purpose of holding it up as a fair representation of the moral condition of St. Louis—for we loudly protest against any such conclusion, and we call upon our fellow-citizens to join us in such protest—but that the immediate actors in the horrid tragedy, may see the work of their hands, and shrink in horror from a repetition of it, and in humble patience seek forgiveness of that community, whose laws they have so outraged,

> and of that God whose image they have, without his permission, wickedly defaced.[32]

It was hardly a sweeping assault on the community, but it was enough to further intensify animosities toward him. In the aftermath of Judge Luke E. Lawless's finding that no one could be charged in the death of McIntosh, Lovejoy felt compelled to move to Alton. Not long after Lawless's ruling, Lovejoy's *Observer* office was ransacked, with another break-in occurring the following week while he was away in Pittsburgh. Vital printing components were stolen or damaged.[33]

In a July column in *The Observer*, Lovejoy ridiculed Lawless's decision. Sadly, he did so by invoking Lawless's Irish heritage and Catholic faith—a clear indication to Lovejoy that Lawless was not disposed to grasp American law or constitutionalism. This troubling aspect of Lovejoy's religious ideology, one where he saw the "cloven foot of Jesuitism" at work in Lawless' decision, speaks to the period's all too frequent and counterintuitive set of principles that might admonish slavery, while simultaneously upholding religious bigotry.[34] Lovejoy's attack on Lawless was returned by a new assault on his press that very evening of publication. It would be the last *Observer* published in St. Louis.[35]

Lovejoy's move to Illinois was hardly well-received. The Illinois legislature issued the following resolution on January 12, 1837:

> *Resolved by the General Assembly of the State of Illinois*, That we highly disapprove of the formation of abolition societies, and of the doctrines promulgated by them. *Resolved*, That the right of property in slaves, is sacred

> to the slave-holding States by the Federal Constitution, and that they cannot be deprived of that right without their consent.[36]

This was the resolution Lincoln protested with his colleague Dan Stone. The two resolutions—one condemning abolitionism, the other slavery—affirmed the precariousness of Lovejoy's position. If there was any agreement among the vast majority of whites in Illinois, irrespective of their views on slavery, it was that abolitionists were part of the problem. Indeed, Missouri was considering its own ban on antislavery publications."[37]

Historian Richard Kielbowicz makes an important distinction concerning the kind of mob violence that took the life of McIntosh, and the kind that harried Lovejoy out of Missouri and ultimately killed him.

> Attacks on antislavery newspapers constituted only a small portion of all antebellum mobbings and only one phase of anti-press violence throughout American history. Still, these mobbings are an especially fruitful source of insights into contending notions of legality in the antebellum era. . . . Abolitionist editors—usually prominent citizens of the same race, ethnicity, and religion as other leading residents—lived among the people who constituted the mobs; hence attacks on abolitionist editors typically involved calculated decisions, elaborate preparation, and public deliberation. In contrast, the most common types of antebellum mobs attacked outsiders or marginal members of the community.[38]

The mob that attacked Lovejoy was made up of intimates—white men whose surface-level ties to Lovejoy heightened their sense of betrayal for his being "leagued with Negroes." The mob that took the life of McIntosh, on the other hand, saw him as a complete outsider, someone who was less than fully human—as suggested by Judge Lawless in his review of the episode. While the fates of McIntosh and Lovejoy were the same, the rationales for the perceived dangers they posed to the community were different.

Today, standing some 300 feet above the Mississippi River, the 110-foot Elijah P. Lovejoy monument in Alton, Illinois, can be easily seen on the drive in from St. Louis. Dedicated in 1897, the base of the monument features four sides dedicated to Lovejoy's life's work. On one side reads his pledge against slavery: "I have sworn eternal opposition to slavery, and by the blessing of God, I will never go back." A little over twenty years after Lovejoy's death, Abraham Lincoln would debate Stephen Douglas for the seventh time in Alton, during their campaign for the Senate. In Alton, Lincoln would insist that the Declaration of Independence included Blacks within its creed that "all men are created equal." If Vicksburg reflected America's desire to cling to its past, Alton came to be emblematic of its willingness to step into the future. As Lincoln said in Alton in 1858, in expressing his opposition to slavery's expansion, "The principle upon which I have insisted in this canvass, is in relation to laying the foundations of new societies."[39] Lincoln would lose the Senate election that year to Douglas, but his vision would win the future. But not before Lovejoy's final act in Alton had played out.

• • •

ELIJAH P. LOVEJOY WAS A KNOWN COMMODITY IN ILLINOIS well before his forced exodus to the state. Beginning in 1832, the *Sangamo Journal* published five articles featuring Lovejoy up until his murder in November of 1837. Lincoln certainly would have been familiar with him, given his close association and interest in the *Journal*. The newspaper's office would before long become Lincoln's "loafing place," where he was drawn to the buzz of activity, while cultivating a strategic position of influence over what was published. William Herndon would describe Lincoln's position at the paper as one of "undisputed control."[40]

In August of 1836, the paper printed a most unusual front-page, three-column article—"published by particular request"—of a speech delivered on the Fourth of July by the abolitionist Presbyterian layman William M. Stewart. Stewart had become one of the most prominent abolitionist leaders in Illinois, if not the nation, and, as early as 1831, was highly critical of the Presbyterian church's failure to denounce slavery.[41] Stewart's speech began by commemorating the sixtieth anniversary of the nation's founding as he outlined the duties of a Christian in properly honoring the blessings bestowed upon them as Americans.

But the speech then pivoted, as Stewart noted that "the story of our beloved country has a dark side to it, and justice requires that it should also be seen." A great challenge facing the nation was that "many of our honored and gifted men, who are flaming republicans, are at this time engaged in the vile practice of buying and selling their fellows for gain." Then Stewart invoked the horrors of the past year:

> Look at Vicksburgh [*sic*] and St. Louis, where men were put to death in a cruel and wanton manner, in direct violation of the laws of the country. True, they were

> charged with gambling and murder, but men must be under a very strong paroxysm of morality who would murder their neighbors to suppress gambling. And on the other side, look at those truly great and excellent men . . . such as Lovejoy: persecuted and driven from place to place, against whom not a shadow of a charge could be brought, except that they were republicans, or in other words, they were lovers of liberty, and like our forefathers were bold and honest enough to speak against tyranny and defend the cause of the poor and oppressed American.[42]

Stewart's speech was a fiery Christian invective against slavery. It linked the murders in Vicksburg to the killing of McIntosh in St. Louis, and to the chastisement of Lovejoy. The arguments were carefully made, though made along the lines of religious objections to slavery and oppression. It was a powerful bromide, to be sure, but it came from an abolitionist—a class of radicals largely detested in the state. That the speech found its way onto the front page of the *Journal* says a great deal about the paper, and perhaps about Lincoln. Indeed, if Lincoln was in any way instrumental in its publication, it would constitute a remarkable, though unsurprising, statement about his own hostility toward slavery. This, of course, would not be the last time key features of Stewart's speech would be presented in the *Journal*, as its structure, moral emphases, and trio of events would be closely aligned with what Lincoln would have to say some eighteen months later.

By the summer of 1837, Lincoln had lost his second love interest, was living on credit in an upstairs room of a general store he shared with the proprietor Joshua Speed, and was getting himself involved in political scuffles with other, more experienced, upward-climbing politicians in Springfield, his new home. "I never saw a sadder face," Speed would recount upon meeting Lincoln.[43] But what would distinguish Lincoln from others who suffered emotionally under the weight of depression was his penchant for broadening the horizon of his personal traumas. Lincoln's move from New Salem to Springfield in 1837 would prove to be a critical event during this truly formative period of his personal and political life.

Lincoln's move to Springfield followed on the heels of his effort to move the state's capital there from Vandalia during the 1836 legislative session that closed in March of 1837. The effort to move the capital was headed by Lincoln, who as leader of the "Long Nine," was thought to have dangled the carrot of patronage related to internal improvements to obtain the critical votes of some legislators. The effort drew accusations of "chicanery and trickery" from one opponent, as Lincoln employed the vaunted tradition of "logrolling"—the legal though, at times, volatile exchange of votes among legislators—to win the day.[44]

The successful vote to move the capital from Vandalia drew the ire of William L. D. Ewing, a pugnacious, chair-throwing (quite literally) legislator who sought to repeal the move in the next legislative session. Lincoln used all of his acerbic wit against Ewing, fueling Ewing's anger and retaliatory inclinations. "Gentlemen, have you no other champion than this coarse and vulgar fellow to bring into the lists against me?" Ewing raged. "Do you suppose that I will descend to break a lance with your low and obscure colleague?"[45] Lincoln immediately responded with a tirade that "nearly tore the hide off Ewing." The repeal effort failed, though Lincoln nearly came to a duel over the episode.[46]

Old State Capitol, Springfield, Illinois.

Personal attacks aside, what were the stakes for Lincoln in moving the capital that were so important that, in the words of historian David Reynolds, Lincoln "came so close to risking his life in its defense?"[47] Reynolds argues that by advocating for a more central, rather than southern, location of the capital (Vandalia is about seventy-five miles south of Springfield), Lincoln sought to move the state's politics to more favorable antislavery ground.[48]

Conversely, Lincoln biographer Michael Burlingame has argued that more practical considerations fueled the move. Vandalia was becoming increasingly remote from the state's more northern population centers; it was susceptible to awful, disease-ridden summers; moreover, roads to the city were frequently impassable. Finally, Vandalia had earned the reputation among its residents as a lawless town, with "brawls and drunken frays in our streets."[49] David Herbert Donald, however, has argued that Lincoln's efforts to move the capital to Springfield drew opposition from proslavery forces in Illinois, who wanted to portray the town as less "sympathetic to the slave states."[50]

It was these anti-Springfield forces who supported the January resolutions in the legislature condemning abolitionist societies.[51] Lincoln and Stone's rebuttal statement in March condemning slavery did not ultimately affect the outcome of the vote to move the capital. Whether intentional or not, Lincoln's leadership in moving the capital to Springfield had implications for the vitality of any antislavery movement in the state. Once finalized, the celebration of the bill's passing to move the capital cost a great deal, as cigars, oysters, and eighty-one bottles of champagne pleased the victorious Sangamon delegation assembled at Capp's Tavern.[52]

On April 15, a twenty-eight-year-old Lincoln arrived in Springfield in less-than-heroic fashion. Arriving on horseback, his life possessions in two saddlebags, he entered Abner Ellis's general store and asked the man behind the counter how much for a single bed, mattress, sheets, and a pillow. Lincoln didn't have the seventeen dollars and had to rely on credit once again. He told the man—one of the proprietors, Joshua Speed—that he planned to earn a living in town as a lawyer. "If I fail in this, I do not know that I could ever pay you."[53] Speed had seen Lincoln speak before and was vaguely familiar with him. Speed offered Lincoln a double bed upstairs they could share. Seeing the stairs, Lincoln took his belongings and left for the room. He wasn't gone long when he returned to the counter and bellowed, "Well, Speed, I am moved!"[54]

Buildings which included Joshua Fry Speed and Abner Ellis's grocery store on the ground floor. Photo courtesy of the Library of Congress.

While Springfield was an alternately muddy, dusty, and hog-infested town of 1600, it was nevertheless several measures up from New Salem culturally speaking. It had more than twenty grocery stores, four hotels, numerous coffee houses, and a new Greek Revival state house to boast of.[55] As he began his sojourn into the city's politics, Lincoln tended to the unfinished business of his courtship with Mary Owens. Upon his arrival in Springfield, Lincoln wrote to her, "I am quite as lonesome here as [I] ever was anywhere in my life."[56] Ultimately, Owens read between the lines of Lincoln's cool letters (he chewed her ear off about mundane politics) and taking matters into her own hands, declined his proposal. Finally spurned, his "vanity deeply wounded," Lincoln reflected on the loss, writing, "I . . . for the first time, began to suspect that I was really a little in love with her."[57] For her part, Owens returned to Kentucky and married in 1838. "Mr. Lincoln was deficient in those little links which make up the chain of woman's happiness," she concluded.[58]

WHILE LINCOLN ADJUSTED TO HIS NEW LIFE IN SPRINGFIELD, controversies were swirling about the increasingly divisive work of Lovejoy in neighboring Missouri.

Lovejoy's newfound passion for abolition marked him out as the worst kind of race-traitor: A zealous and articulate opponent of slavery who sided with the likes of McIntosh over the law-abiding and God-fearing white citizens of St. Louis. By October 1837, Lovejoy's press had been destroyed, his home broken into, and his life under a constant state of threat. In a letter recounting an attack he suffered at his in-laws' home after a sermon he delivered in St. Charles, Missouri, Lovejoy came face to face with the power of racial conspiracy:

> They were armed with pistols and dirks [a kind of dagger], and one pistol was discharged, whether at any person or not, I did not know. The fellow from Mississippi seemed the most bent on my destruction. He did not appear at all drunken, but both in words and actions manifested the most fiendish malignity of feeling and purpose. He was telling a story to the mobites, which, whether true or false (I know not), was just calculated to madden them. His story was that his wife had lately been violated by a negro. And this he said was all owing to me, who had instigated the negro to do the deed. He was a ruined man, he said, had just as lief die as not; but before he died, he "would have my blood."[59]

Lovejoy and his family fended off several more attacks that evening before fleeing. He thereafter kept "a loaded musket near the bed as he slept."[60]

These violent confrontations spoke to underlying fears of racial "amalgamation" that would presumably come with emancipation. Abolition was the path to sexual relations between Blacks and whites—a fear articulated by Thomas Jefferson in 1781, when in answering the question, "Why not retain and incorporate the blacks into the state?" in his *Notes on the State of Virginia*, he compared American slavery to that of ancient Rome. "Among the Romans, emancipation required but one effort," Jefferson wrote. "The slave, when made free, might mix with, without staining the blood of his master. But with us a second is necessary, unknown to history. When freed, he is to be removed beyond the reach of mixture."[61] Part of the historic support among whites for colonization was its removal of the problem of interracial mixing. Short of that, abolition was seen by many Southerners as tacit support for "miscegenation."

It was a charge that would later be hurled at Lincoln by Stephen Douglas in their fourth debate in 1858, when Douglass accused Lincoln of supporting interracial marriage. "I do not understand that, because I do not want a negro woman for a slave, I must necessarily want her for a wife," Lincoln said to cheers and laughter. "My understanding is that I can just let her alone. I am now in my fiftieth year, and I certainly never have had a black woman for either a slave or a wife. So it seems to me quite possible for us to get along without making either slaves or wives of negroes."[62] While this retort scored political points for Lincoln at the time, his failure to endorse complete social equality became a source of criticism over the years. His rejection of slavery did not include the immediate support for Black liberation.

For his part, Lovejoy soldiered on, planning an antislavery convention with abolitionist Edward Beecher in Springfield, Illinois, in the weeks following the assault at St. Charles.[63] There was much debate over whether or not the increasingly imperiled Lovejoy should move *The Observer* to another, safer city. In what would prove to be his last public speech before his murder, Lovejoy rejected the prospect outright. "Why should I flee from Alton?" he said. "Is this not a free state?"

> You may hang me up, as the mob hung up the individuals at Vicksburgh [*sic*]! You may burn me at the stake, as they did McIntosh at St. Louis; or you tar and feather me, or throw me in the Mississippi, as you have often threatened to do; but you cannot disgrace me.... It is because I fear God that I am not afraid of all who oppose me in this city. No, sir, the contest has commenced here; and here it must be finished. Before God and you all, I here pledge myself to continue it, if need be, til death. If I fall, my grave shall be made in Alton.[64]

Just as William M. Stewart did in his July 4 speech in 1836, Lovejoy connected the struggle of emancipation to the deaths of Vicksburg's gamblers and Francis McIntosh.

On the morning of November 7, 1837, the *Missouri Fulton* was en route along the Mississippi River to Alton, Illinois, from St. Louis. One of its significant pieces of cargo was Lovejoy's new printing press.[65] It arrived safely in the wee hours of the morning at a warehouse, where Lovejoy awaited it, along with armed guards prepared to defend it. But by the end of the day, a drunken mob had assembled outside the warehouse. In time, some two hundred men surrounded the place and exchanged fire with the men inside, whose number included Alton's mayor. After much chaos, a fire on the roof was started by one of the mob, forcing Lovejoy and the storekeeper to exit the warehouse. Lovejoy was struck immediately by a volley of five shots. He somehow managed to reenter the building and clamber upstairs to the second floor where, "clutching his chest," he spoke his final words: "Oh, God, I am shot."[66] The mob would find the press and carry it to the Mississippi, where they shattered it and tossed its remains into the river. Lovejoy had died, just two days before his thirty-fifth birthday, as he said he might—in Alton, a victim of a mob not unlike the one that ended the lives of those lynched in Vicksburg, or Francis McIntosh, whose death catalyzed his own end.

Lovejoy's death sparked a national outrage that would burn for decades. Lincoln had been following the events in St. Louis for some time and may well have coauthored an editorial in the *Sangamo Journal* on June 30, 1836, condemning the mob's destruction of Lovejoy's press.[67] But the *Journal*, like many other newspapers in the region, was largely silent on the subject of Lovejoy's murder in the ensuing weeks, covering the murder in the next edition, but little more. Those newspapers that did cover Lovejoy's killing tended to cast blame on the abolitionists themselves instead of on the mob. The tempestuous climate cast a cautionary pall over regional presses, who for obvious reasons decided that covering the Lovejoy murder might invite unwelcome scrutiny.[68] Indeed, the *Sangamo Journal* made no reference to Lovejoy's murder again until February 3, 1838, when Lincoln would weigh in on the last thousand days' events.[69]

The Shooting of Elijah P. Lovejoy,
American Anti-Slavery Almanac, *1839*.

Northern newspapers did cover Lovejoy's murder, however, and his death inspired abolitionists like Wendell Phillips, who defended Lovejoy's actions before a large and contentious audience in Boston in December of 1837. "Welcome the despotism of the Sultan," Phillips told the crowd gathered at Faneuil Hall, "where one knows what he may publish and what he may not, rather than the tyranny of this many-headed monster, the mob, where we know not what we may do or say, till some fellow-citizen has tried it, and paid for the lesson with his life."[70] William Lloyd Garrison's *Liberator* likewise supported Lovejoy and his antislavery cause. In December of 1837, the *Liberator*'s front page was strewn with national press coverage of Lovejoy's death, including a reprint from the *Fitchburg Courier*, which read, "[Lovejoy] has fallen a victim to the wicked spirit of slavery—a martyr to the cause of human rights, of freedom of speech, and of the Press."[71] It was a statement which Garrison only partly agreed with, as he deemed Lovejoy to be unworthy of the term martyr, because he chose to arm himself. Edward Beecher disagreed. "It is said he died with murderous weapons in his hand, and with the blood of a fellow being on them. This is false. He died in defense of justice, and of the law, and of right: and with the instrument of justice in his hands."[72]

In addition to inspiring abolitionists (radicalizing, might be the better word in the case of John Brown, who, in the aftermath of Lovejoy's murder, "consecrated his life to the destruction of slavery"),[73] Lovejoy's death deeply moved transcendentalists like Ralph Waldo Emerson and Henry David Thoreau. As Janet Kemper Beck has written, Lovejoy's murder "drove Emerson in November of 1837 to break his long silence and address the slavery question publicly for the first time."[74] In a speech at the Second Church in Concord, Emerson chastised Boston's citizens gathered at a lyceum meeting, saying, "Even the platform of the lyceum, hitherto the freest of all organs, is bandaged and muffled that it threatens to be silent."[75] Lincoln would prove to be among a small group across the nation to be moved enough by Lovejoy's death to speak out, and perhaps the only elected official to do so.

Like McIntosh's killers, Lovejoy's would go unpunished. It was a sign that vigilantism was becoming an alarmingly successful competitor with the law. Unlike the transcendentalists who would frequently invoke a "higher" law in their writings, Lincoln would always be careful to acknowledge that despite the presence of "bad" laws, they were to be adhered to until changed through proper channels. Years later, in an 1842 address at the Washington Temperance Society, Lincoln advocated for persuasion, rather than condemnation, as the path toward curing the ills of alcoholism in society. "In my judgment, such of us as have never fallen victims, have been spared more from the absence of appetite, than from any mental or moral superiority over those who have," Lincoln said.[76] As he would eloquently refuse to judge Southerners for their support of slavery in his Second Inaugural Address, here Lincoln refused to take the position of a purist on the question of alcoholism. With respect to abolitionism, Lincoln reasoned that the failure to understand the viewpoint of slaveholders didn't mitigate against the inherent wrong of slavery; rather, it made it a wrong more difficult to right because of sanctimoniousness.

In one of history's poignant developments, it was Elijah's brother Owen Lovejoy who would, in 1854, invite Abraham Lincoln to attend the nascent Republican Party's convention in Illinois. According to Lovejoy biographers William F. Moore and Jane Ann Moore, Lincoln was "leery of [Owen] Lovejoy's reputation as a fanatical abolitionist."[77] Nevertheless, the two would forge an important friendship, one with considerable political consequences, as "Lovejoy's work was instrumental in securing [Illinois] for Lincoln in the 1860 presidential election."[78]

For decades, Lovejoy's murder in Alton came to symbolize the great divide over slavery and the violent assault on liberty. As Wendell Phillips wrote in 1867, after paying a visit to Alton and Lovejoy's old office and the warehouse where he was killed:

> I can never forget the quick, sharp agony of that hour which brought us the news of Lovejoy's death. We had not fully learned the bloodthirstiness of the slave power. When John Brown confronted it at Harpers Ferry, we knew and had long known the risk any man ran who defied the fiend. But twenty years before, Garrison had just walked up to its horrors, and we saw it but blindly.

> The gun fired at Lovejoy was like that of Sumter—it shattered a world of dreams.[79]

THE KILLING OF ELIJAH P. LOVEJOY WAS THE THIRD ACT IN A grave political drama Lincoln saw unfolding across the country. The lynchings in Mississippi in the summer of 1835 were first. Initiated by rumors over a slave revolt and genuine hatred for a class of men deemed morally unfit, it led to a series of indiscriminate killings of both Blacks and whites. The following April saw the killing of Francis McIntosh, pulled from his jail cell and burned before hundreds of St. Louis citizens. The third and final mob killing that drew Lincoln's attention was the shooting of Lovejoy in 1837. Nearly twenty years later, in an 1857 letter written to his friend Rev. James Lemen, Lincoln said, "Lovejoy's tragic death for freedom in every sense marked his sad ending as the most important single event that ever happened in the new world."[80] Nearly a thousand days had transpired between the first killings and Lincoln's speech at Springfield's Baptist Church, in January of 1838, where he put the three sets of murders on the Mississippi in a larger political context.

Was Lovejoy's murder "the most important single event that ever happened in the new world" as Lincoln wrote, or the equivalent of the firing upon Fort Sumter that began the Civil War, as Wendell Phillips suggested? Both seem exaggerated though noble gestures to a grim moment in American history. And yet, Lovejoy's life and death did become highly symbolic of an abolitionist movement growing increasingly radical, one that insisted upon immediate emancipation. Wendell Phillips, Ralph Waldo Emerson, John Brown, and yes, Abraham Lincoln, among many others, were all deeply moved by the story of Alton, Illinois.

A few months after the murder of Lovejoy, Lincoln would speak before Springfield's Young Men's Lyceum at the town's Baptist church a few blocks from where he lived. The stories of Vicksburg, St. Louis, and Alton would become important and interconnected parts of a chain of events that evoked a sense of dread in the twenty-eight-year-old Lincoln, events that he spoke to in the moment like no other elected official at the time. He had delivered impromptu speeches before, along with speeches before his colleagues in the General Assembly. But now, he would prepare a comprehensive address—not just on banks, or canals, or public credit—but on the grim direction of the country. And he knew it would be published for all to see. Whether in his failed relationship with Mary Owens, or in his move to Springfield, or in his beginnings as a lawyer, Lincoln had spent the better part of 1837 searching for a new start. Tormented as he was in his personal life, Abraham Lincoln was now preparing to address the torments of a nation steadily falling into chaos.

FOUR

1838: TRANSFORMATION

It was already dark by the time Lincoln would have left his second-floor room at Joshua Speed's store to begin the five-minute walk down to the Baptist church, some two blocks east before turning right on Seventh Street. January 27, 1838, was the kind of cold winter day with an early sunset that contributed to Lincoln's melancholy. While the speech he would present would only take about twenty-five minutes to deliver, it would have profound implications for understanding the politics that would drive Lincoln for the next twenty-five years. In the words of William Herndon, who knew him well, and whose father had served with Lincoln as part of the "Long Nine" in the Illinois legislature, the speech "in point of rhetorical effort . . . excels anything he ever afterward attempted."[1]

He did not have an optimistic message. Elijah P. Lovejoy's death brought home quite literally to Lincoln the accelerating national trend of mob violence. While the lynching spree that began in July of 1835 was in far-off Mississippi, the burning of Francis McIntosh in April of 1836 was in neighboring Missouri. Now, with Lovejoy's shooting in downstate Alton, Illinois, in

November of 1837, the time for Lincoln to add his voice to the discussion over what to do about the antidemocratic forces threatening American democracy had come. The mob was now at his doorstep. But what to say about it?

The discussion Lincoln threw himself into had been mostly one-sided. Few besides those in the abolitionist movement viewed these recent episodes as unpleasant. Most whites saw them as necessary responses to Black rebellion or criminality. And the murder of Vicksburg's gamblers was connected to the threat of insurrection. As for the other whites Mississippians killed, they were the recipients of justice for their perceived assistance in the conspiracy. Lovejoy, too, was part of the collateral damage inflicted upon those whites who took it upon themselves to side with Blacks in their brutish efforts to upend the social order.

But Lincoln did not side with the conspiracists. He chose instead to convey the inherent danger presented to America's constitutional order by these extrajudicial killings. This did not make Lincoln an abolitionist. But by extending sympathy to falsely accused African Americans, as risky an enterprise as that was, he found common ground with them. Lincoln certainly could have considered other cases in making his point—those less directly tied to race and American slavery. In fact, the *Sangamo Journal* presented a string of such cases in its August 29, 1835, edition. "The state of society is awful," the article began. "Brute force has superseded the law at many places, and violence become the 'order of the day.'" The episodes outlined in the report included "base murders on the Baltimore rail roads," the "conflagration of the Ursuline convent"—the burning down of a Catholic convent by a Protestant mob in Charlestown, Massachusetts, a year earlier—and a set of mob-led executions in Mississippi, unrelated to the Murrell "excitement" that began in Vicksburg.[2] These—and other such examples—offered ample cover for Lincoln to make his case, while avoiding third-rail politics in racially conservative Illinois. Lincoln's contemporaries certainly took this route.

Lincoln's speech at the Young Men's Lyceum, held at Springfield's Baptist Church, was succeeded by two other, far more cautious addresses. Historian Angela G. Ray's research has brought to light twenty-three-year-old Antrim Campbell's February Lyceum Address, just three weeks after Lincoln's, along with the twenty-two-year-old James C. Conkling's speech, delivered about a year later. Read alongside Lincoln's address, we can see similarities in theme, while also recognizing the cautious departures Lincoln's colleagues took.

Campbell's speech employed the flowery and romantic language familiar to the time. His subject—the value of education, especially in history, for improving the quality of public opinion—was likewise common to the era. Campbell flattered his audience by arguing that voluntary civic associations such as lyceums "are nurseries from whence spring forests of political timber to strengthen and beautify our national edifice."[3] He then traced the misuse of ambition—"the noblest gift of the Creator to mankind"—from ancient Greece to modern times, driving home his point that understanding the fall of democratic institutions, and therefore the risks to our own, requires a close reading of history. "Her history," Campbell said, referring to Greece, "should be profoundly studied by every American who feels interested in the permanence of our institutions."[4]

Whether the word employed was "permanence," as in Campbell's address, or "perpetuation," as used in the title of Lincoln's, there was clearly an abiding interest in shoring up democratic institutions in America at the time. Campbell was not cribbing from Lincoln's speech, any more than Lincoln stole from the abolitionist William M. Stewart's July Fourth Address in 1836. Fear of losing the gift of republican government was part of the spirit of the age. As Garry Wills has noted, the "Greek Revival" of the nineteenth century influenced everything from American architecture to poetry. More relevant to politics was a renewed attentiveness to the virtue of "the people," a departure from the eighteenth century's emphasis on republicanism and the virtue of representatives.[5]

"Our lot is cast in turbulent times," Campbell said, nearing the end of his address. "The waves of discord are rolling with an angry tumult over the face of our Republic." Like Lincoln, Campbell embraced a generational "responsibility to preserve inviolate these blessings of civil and religious liberty, and transmit them unimpaired to our posterity." Campbell finished his speech with a romantic flourish. "May we perform that duty nobly, and when the portals of the mysterious grave shall open to receive this mortal coil, and our spirits shall be washed to purer, holier realms, may we possess the peaceful, calm, self-ennobling assurance, that ours has been a faithful and acceptable service."[6]

The language of duty, nobly performed, calls to mind Lincoln at Gettysburg, as the washing of spirits may remind those familiar with Lincoln's 1854 speech at Peoria, Illinois, of America's soiled republican robe in need of cleansing. The familiar language suggests Lincoln was singing from the same hymn book as his contemporaries, but with a clearer and stronger voice. Lincoln's Peoria speech opposing the Kansas–Nebraska Act captured an enduring three-fold theme of his youth, one first articulated at the Lyceum: America has lost its way; she must repent;

and she must return to first principles. At Peoria, the refrain would become, "Our republican robe is soiled, and trailed in the dust. Let us repurify it. Let us turn and wash it white in the spirit if not the blood of the Revolution."[7] The key distinction between Lincoln's language and that used by his contemporaries was the degree of urgency and specificity he employed in driving home his point. And most significantly, Lincoln did not avoid the turbulent subject of race.

James C. Conkling's Lyceum speech a year later is another good example. While Conkling undertook a historical and comparative assessment of public education and civilizational development (he had surprisingly positive things to say about African history, for the time), his attention to mob violence in America lacked the directness and specificity of Lincoln.[8] Conkling's sweeping historical meditation—the *Sangamon Journal* had to publish the text of the speech over two editions—concluded with his admiration for societies like the Lyceum, where the rudiments of popular government could be taught. "Five thousand are now scattered through the land," Conkling said in praise of the lyceums, "and experience leads us to conclude that from these will arise our future philosophers, our statesmen, and our orators." The need to produce such men was not academic for Conkling, for such "pure disinterested patriots . . . will stand firm to their posts in this hour of danger—who will resist the insidious attacks of internal foes, as well as the open aggressions of declared enemies—who will stem the tide of popular fury, and oppose their breasts as a barrier to its rage."[9]

Angela Ray summarized the relationship between these three Lyceum speeches well.

> Of course, despite the similarities between the lectures, the three men made their claims in different ways. Reading the lectures side by side offers considerable scope for understanding addresses to the Young Men's Lyceum generally and Lincoln's address specifically. For whereas the three lectures were highly conventional—Lincoln's included—variations both subtle and overt create the grounds for arguing that Lincoln's lecture was more pointed and bold than the others. The lectures varied in the treatment of recurring themes: of the relationship between generations, the role of passion and reason in public life, and the question of national survival.[10]

To grasp just how bold Lincoln's address was, we must revisit the speech comprehensively—and in doing so, note the similarities and crucial differences found in another speech given by one of Lincoln's contemporaries—William Stewart. Stewart's address, as briefly touched on in the last chapter, presented a radical religious assault on slavery. Yet it was Lincoln's more subtle and masterfully tailored secular speech that was designed to speak to the whole of America.

ASIDE FROM THE NEWSPAPER'S SIGNATURE IMAGE OF A HAND pointing to the notice near the bottom right-hand corner of the second page, there was nothing special about the *Sangamo Journal*'s announcement of Abraham Lincoln's talk for the night of January 27, 1838.

> THE YOUNG MEN'S LYCEUM will meet at the usual time and place. In compliance with the request of the Lyceum, A. LINCOLN, Esq. will deliver an Address to the members of that body on Saturday evening the 27th inst. The public are invited to attend.
>
> By order of the Lyceum. JH Matheny, Sec'y.[11]

Those in the know knew to show up at the Baptist church on Seventh and Adams Streets between "half past six or seven o'clock."[12] We have no record of how many people attended that evening, but any anticipation for a Saturday night lecture on "The Perpetuation of Our Political Institutions," in mid-winter Illinois no less, speaks to the popularity of the Lyceum gatherings at the time. Only in recent months had the *Sangamo Journal* advertised that women were also welcome to attend, a sign of a developing women's movement, and the broad interest lyceums were drawing.

As suggested in Conkling's speech, lyceums became a kind of cultural phenomenon in nineteenth century America, spreading not only the skill and appreciation for public debate, but also serving as national repositories for disseminating information of social and political importance. If mob violence reflected the darker side of American expansion in the age of Jackson, lyceums reflected the period's enthusiasm for democratic enlightenment.[13] Still relatively new to Springfield, Lincoln grasped the significance of participating in a forum "for up-and-coming men to come together and practice the forms of civic engagement in a pleasurable, clublike setting."[14] Conkling's estimate was right—by the time Lincoln delivered his address in Springfield, the number of lyceums around the nation approached five thousand, becoming particularly popular intellectual venues in the American West.[15]

Because Lincoln was but a twice-elected representative in the state legislature at the time and not a statewide officeholder, let alone president, neither his notes nor the original document of the Lyceum Address have been preserved. While it was Lincoln's first public speech of consequence, one that would outline his views on the dominant subjects of the day, it was not viewed as particularly significant at the time. The *Sangamo Journal*'s transcription, provided by Lincoln, is as close to an original text as we will likely ever get. Likewise, there is no real record of how his speech was delivered, nor of his audience's response. The fixtures we have come to associate with Lincoln's oratory—the high-pitched voice, the head nods, and the hands stuffed deep into his pockets—these we can only imagine for the Lyceum. There is no grainy, hatless photo, as was miraculously discovered for his Gettysburg Address, to serve our imaginations; the Lyceum predated the age of photography. We cannot know what he wore or who he visited with before the talk as we do at Cooper Union, for instance, with details that help us "see" Lincoln, a person already presented to us all-too-marbled-over in history.[16] At the Lyceum, all we have are Lincoln's words.

What we do have, thanks to the work of historians, is a feel for the politics of Springfield, along with a record of other Lyceum speeches and similar addresses at the time. These provide valuable guides for seeing the darker and more prophetic side of Lincoln's early political thought. As we know, Lincoln was not the only Illinois politician to issue dire warnings about the fate of America. In November of 1837, just a few months before his speech, one of the topics of the Lyceum was "Do the signs of the present times indicate the downfall of America?"[17] If Lincoln's bleak assessment of the times was not entirely unique, what then distinguished his Lyceum speech from others?

William M. Stewart's July Fourth Address of 1836 offers important insights into debates over slavery, the relevance of America's founding to the 1830s, and the underlying fears of the erosion of democracy. Published in the *Sangamo Journal* on August 29, Stewart's speech is a kind of foreshadowing of Lincoln's Lyceum Address. Indeed, the similarities are striking. Stewart begins with a "debt of gratitude" on the sixtieth anniversary of independence, noting that Americans "have enjoyed more liberty and greater privileges than the people of any other nation."[18]

Stewart then turns to the duties of a Christian toward one's country, with a particular view toward upholding the law. "Mobs, tumults, and insurrections are alike contrary to the good of the community, the spirit of our free institutions, and the religion of the Bible," Stewart asserted.[19] How should Christians prevent such assaults on the community? Education is the answer. "To parents and those who have the care of children and youths," Stewart says, "I would say, as you love your country, teach the 'fear of god, which is the beginning of wisdom,' and also the first principles of government, that 'all men are born free and equal.' Teach them to regard the rights of others, and to observe the strictest rules of justice and honor in their dealings with mankind."[20]

As discussed, Stewart acknowledges "our beloved country has a dark side to it," as he pivots toward condemning the horrible crimes committed in "Vicksburgh and St. Louis."[21] These cases are windows into the evils of slavery, according to Stewart, and they serve as a warning for the loss of one's humanity in ignoring them. "Our government cannot be sustained without virtue and intelligence; these cannot be sustained without Christian religion, nor this without the Bible," he says, nearing his conclusion. Fittingly, he closes his address with a prayer: "That God may bless you and this nation, with peace and great prosperity at home; and with deserved honor for wisdom and justice abroad, is the prayer of your fellow citizen."[22]

If there was a singular fear among America's founders—call it an obsession, if you like—it was the question of self-government's durability. One sees it again and again in Lincoln's greatest speeches: an unwavering attentiveness to the "task" of passing on the blessings of free government. Here, with Stewart, the familiar obsession is present, though the remedy is different. Stewart's solution is biblical rather than secular instruction. We are called to liberty and equality through an adherence to God's words first—not those of the Constitution. Lincoln's challenge at the Lyceum was to, in some ways, take the idea of equality and equal justice under the law out of the religious context that abolitionists had framed it, and to make it part of our "civil religion."

When Lincoln famously began his Gettysburg Address with "Four score and seven years ago," he conjured up the Revolution and Declaration, activating the "great task remaining before us." In other words, the American founding represented an implicit challenge to all subsequent generations. But what should not be overlooked is that Lincoln had been cultivating these ideas for twenty-five years. In effect, the Gettysburg Address streamlined and polished the sentiments Lincoln first meaningfully expressed at the Lyceum. However laboriously Lincoln laid them out in Springfield in 1838, they are there:

> We find ourselves under the government of a system of political institutions, conducing more essentially to the ends of civil and religious liberty, than any of which

> the history of former times tells us. We, when mounting the stage of existence, found ourselves the legal inheritors of these fundamental blessings. We toiled not in the acquirement or establishment of them—they are a legacy bequeathed us, by a *once* hardy, brave, and patriotic, but *now* lamented and departed race of ancestors.[23]

At Gettysburg, this was boiled down to: "Four score and seven years ago our fathers brought forth on this continent a new nation, conceived in liberty, and dedicated to the proposition that all men are created equal."[24] While Lincoln at Gettysburg lamented the dead and dying generation of men killed during the Civil War, at the Lyceum in 1838, he was lamenting a "departed race of ancestors"—the founding generation whom Lincoln labeled "our fathers," as he would at Gettysburg ("Our fathers brought forth on this continent . . .").[25]

Later in the Lyceum, Lincoln implored that the Declaration of Independence, the Constitution, and laws of the nation should "become the political religion of the nation."[26] And if even civil religion requires prayer, Lincoln suggested a familiar "Our Father(s)" beginning. This religious thread invoking what is sacred in the secular arena of politics has culminating moments in Lincoln's greatest speeches: at both the conclusion of the Gettysburg Address, where an implicit oath is required ("we here highly resolve that these dead shall not have died in vain"), and at the end of the Second Inaugural Address ("With malice toward none with charity for all with firmness in the right as God gives us to see the right, let us strive on to finish the work we are in").[27]

I will come to Lincoln's mysterious conclusion to the Lyceum Address later in this chapter, but for now, it's worth emphasizing that, in his very first speech of broad political insight, Lincoln established a template that would serve him for the remainder of his life. America's form of government is a gift; it was given to us by a founding generation unmatched in America's history; and finally, each generation is charged with protecting the sacred edifice of self-government it has inherited. Lincoln uses the word "task" four times at the Lyceum. Like his contemporaries, his fixation is on solving the problem of a growing indifference to the rule of law. If Lincoln is to be seen as a moderate—a word too imprecise and overused in defining his politics—then the moderating influence upon him is his interest in problem-solving. Moderates are seldom radical; pragmatists often are. Where the former looks to keep order or "harmony," the pragmatist is more interested in resolution—and that may require a more radical, unsettling form of politics. We will see that when Lincoln does the immoderate thing at the Lyceum—namely when he invokes slavery and race.

LINCOLN'S OPENING PARAGRAPH AT THE LYCEUM IS NEARLY the length of the Gettysburg Address, at 236 words. But its familiar themes of reverence for the founding generation and honoring their sacrifice with our own are all there. So too is his intriguing consideration for humanity outside America's borders. Like Jefferson's "decent respect for the opinion of mankind" written in the Declaration of Independence seeks a global audience, Lincoln wants to establish the mission of self-government as a human endeavor, rather than a strictly American one. The last two words of the Gettysburg Address are "the earth"; the final two words of the Second Inaugural are "all nations." At the Lyceum, Lincoln concludes his opening statement by stating:

"This task of gratitude to our fathers, justice to ourselves, duty to posterity, and *love for our species in general*, all imperatively require us faithfully to perform."[28] From the very beginning—and the Lyceum has no rival in this regard with respect to his rhetoric—Lincoln wove an international, humanitarian-aspiring objective into his political thought. This shouldn't be confused with Woodrow Wilson's call to "make the world safe for democracy." At the Lyceum, Lincoln is first trying to make *America* safe for democracy.

The perils of democratic life can be seen in those whom Lincoln chooses to name in his text. Napoleon is mentioned twice, along with Alexander the Great and Julius Caesar. These are the dangerously ambitious men to be feared at times when democracy is imperiled. The only two Americans Lincoln refers to in the address are Francis McIntosh—a victim of unchecked antidemocratic passions—and George Washington, the personification of the republican ideal. Lincoln historians rightly emphasize Lincoln's affection for Washington from his childhood, when he became acquainted with him in Mason Locke Weems's biography *The Life of George Washington*. It was one of the literary staples he would return to again and again.[29]

At Gettysburg, Lincoln would center his message around the promises of the Declaration and its creed of equality. The "new birth of freedom" required extending Jefferson and the founders' promise to all. But even Lincoln recognized that the majority of his countrymen did not view Blacks as their equals—and many could and did perceive this to be in no ways in conflict with the Declaration or the nation's ideals. This would require a transvaluation of values, a complete reorienting of what whites believed about their relationship to African Americans. Yet, at the Lyceum, Lincoln centered Washington, who was not only a figure of national unity, but the antithesis of the tyrants he had mentioned.

This is because Washington was, and is, best known for what he didn't do, as much as for what he did. It is easy, for example, to imagine Alexander the Great, Julius Caesar, or Napoleon Bonaparte crossing the Delaware River or defeating the British forces at Yorktown. It is unimaginable, however, to consider any of them relinquishing power as Washington did. In an era marked by the absence of restraint, it was Washington's example of self-abnegation that Lincoln looked for, not his leadership on the battlefield or even as president. As a Whig, Lincoln was highly critical of the leadership model presented to the nation by Andrew Jackson in the years preceding the Lyceum Address. The traits by which Jackson was defined (certainly by his political opponents)—hubris, defiance, and intemperance—were the very ones that Lincoln was hoping to see exorcised from the body politic in 1838.

As he argues later in the speech, similar personal failings with national implications such as "jealousy, envy, and avarice" were mitigated during the Revolutionary era by the fact that prestige and honor were associated with their absence from one's character—at least in politics. The dying off of the "fathers" meant the dissolution of this esteemed example they set for conducting politics. The effect was very much connected to the behavior of ordinary citizens, who were presently lacking the personal memory and experience with the virtues of republicanism and thus returning to their natural self-interested impulses. The mob, after all, reflects lessons taught to them by those who govern them. When Herman Melville has Starbuck, the first mate of the *Pequod*, ponder the effects of Captain Ahab's abuses in *Moby-Dick*, he posits: "Say'st all of us are

Ahabs. Great God forbid!"[30] Like the biblical King Ahab, who was cut off from Naboth's ancestral blessings, Melville suggests, in his own way, that mid-nineteenth-century Americans may well have been cut off from a blessed ancestral line as well. Such is the fate of Ahabs. On this score, Lincoln and Melville are tapping the same spiritual vein of politics.[31] Our wise instructors have died off.

THE MOST MEMORABLE LINE FROM THE LYCEUM ADDRESS warns Americans of a future premised upon the failure to meet the challenge of lawlessness. As Thurston Clarke noted in his book on John F. Kennedy's Inaugural Address, JFK's famous line, "*And so my fellow Americans, ask not what your country can do for you, ask what you can do for your country*," was the master sentence of that memorable speech. It inspired a generation of Americans to enter politics and make sacrifices that they otherwise would not have made. As Clarke says, Kennedy's "master sentence"—the one to which the entire purpose of the speech is unlocked—was designed to join "Roosevelt's 'the only thing we have to fear is fear itself' and Lincoln's 'With malice toward none; with charity for all.'"[32]

If there is one such intended sentence in Lincoln's Lyceum Address, we cannot know; the speech's construction and any related notes remain a mystery. But the one sentence historians have turned to most often, the one documentarian Ken Burns culled for his famed Civil War documentary, is this final one in the early sequence in the speech:

> At what point shall we expect the approach of danger? By what means shall we fortify against it?— Shall

> we expect some transatlantic military giant, to step the Ocean, and crush us at a blow? Never!—All the armies of Europe, Asia, and Africa combined, with all the treasure of the earth (our own excepted) in their military chest; with a Buonaparte for a commander, could not, by force, take a drink from the Ohio, or make a track on the Blue Ridge, in a trial of a thousand years.
>
> At what point then is the approach of danger to be expected? I answer, if it ever reach us, it must spring up amongst us. It cannot come from abroad. If destruction be our lot, we must ourselves be its author and finisher. *As a nation of freemen, we must live through all time, or die by suicide.*[33]

Historians have been drawn to the harshness of this final line—and for good reason. As already discussed, the theme of America's endangered political institutions was a common one for the period, including the speeches delivered at the Lyceum in the months before and after Lincoln's address. But it is Lincoln who applies the graphic warning of suicide. It is a hard-hitting line—certainly for a man familiar with suicidal thoughts—that captures with ghastly precision what failure to adhere to the nation's laws will lead to.

The collapse of republics as an obsession of the founders was acutely indulged by James Madison, whose political theory found in the *Federalist Papers* sought to address the failings of Republican states. Indeed, many of the founders had combed over the English historian Edward Gibbon's *Decline and Fall of the Roman Empire*, published in the same year as the Declaration of Independence.[34] Concern over the decline and ultimate failure of self-government was so prevalent among the founding generation in the early American republic that, whether apocryphal or not, one is inclined to assume Benjamin Franklin believed the response he is purported to have uttered at the conclusion of the Constitutional Convention in 1787, when asked what kind of government Americans could expect. "A republic," he is famously said to have replied. "If you can keep it."[35]

Keeping the republic is one kind of call to arms; avoiding killing it is another. Lincoln's line about suicide has the dint of prophecy because of its implicit warning against national hubris and self-delusion. The abandonment of all that is good is the byproduct of a frenzied and passion-fueled spirit. If a republic can be lost, as Franklin suggested, then it is because the people lose themselves first, according to Lincoln. This is the very heart of civic republicanism's political thought: Only a people fit to govern themselves *personally* can be fit to practice self-government *politically*.

Ironically, as Madison biographer Jack Rakove has observed, Madison "[rejected] the classical axiom that made the civic virtue of its citizens the sustaining strength of a republic."[36] Where Madison extolled the wisdom of an extended and compound (federal) republic to weaken the "mischiefs of faction" in Federalist 10, Lincoln sought to restore the classical model. Personal restraint had to be a fundamental characteristic of a republic's citizens, even where checks and balances and a separation of powers were present. For Lincoln, the Constitution's external devices were no longer a match for the inner maladies driving human ambition.

Lincoln did not so much disapprove of Madison's framework for a constitution that addressed the regression toward mob rule in Republican states. The Constitution's supremacy was to become a guiding light for Lincoln over the course of his presidency.[37] But Madison's belief that "had every Athenian citizen been a Socrates, every Athenian assembly would still have been a mob" goes too far for Lincoln. Lincoln's warning against national suicide is predicated upon the belief that civic virtue can be taught; that the collective will of the people needn't redound to chaos or avarice. This is enshrined most poignantly at Gettysburg, where Lincoln's vision is for a world where "government of the people, by the people, for the people, shall not perish from the earth."

This faith in the people to practice virtue that enables self-government is a rebuke to Madison in Federalist 51, where he opines, "A dependence on the people is, no doubt, the primary control on the government; but experience has taught mankind the necessity of auxiliary precautions."[38] One of the great lessons drawn by Lincoln from the experience of the 1830s was the need to return to first principles. Mob violence did not prove the inability of the people to rule themselves successfully, for Lincoln; it rather underscored the imperative to foster a society where self-mastery and public virtue were more deeply ingrained. The "Perpetuation of Our Political Institutions," the formal title of Lincoln's talk, could therefore only be won by a reverence for them, premised upon first improving the quality of the people and their character.

Readers of the Lyceum Address may be forgiven some for considering Lincoln's attention to the character of the nation's citizenship as somewhat of a bait and switch for a speech on the perpetuation of America's political institutions. There's not much of any discussion of institutions, save for Lincoln's consideration of America's courts. Given the events over the thousand days preceding the Lyceum speech, there was good reason for Lincoln to focus attention on the nation's courts.

Lincoln mentions the courts twice at the Lyceum. The first time is early in the address when he says, "I hope I am over wary," concerning the rise of mob violence, "but if I am not, there is, even now, something of ill-omen, amongst us. I mean the increasing disregard for law which pervades the country; the growing disposition to substitute the wild and furious passions, in lieu of the sober judgment of Courts." The second time he invokes the judicial branch of government in the middle of the speech, where he says:

> Let reverence for the laws, be breathed by every American mother, to the lisping babe, that prattles on her lap—let it be taught in schools, in seminaries, and in colleges; let it be written in Primers, spelling books, and in Almanacs;—let it be preached from the pulpit, proclaimed in legislative halls, and enforced in courts of justice.[39]

"Enforced in courts of justice" is an odd turn of phrase. It seems to fly in the face of the separation of powers ingrained in America's political system, where the enforcement of the laws belongs to the executive branch of government. Yet we may see some premonitions of this line of reasoning in recent politics, where the executive branch has been the chief source of political chaos and mob-incitement. What to do in that circumstance? Americans concerned over the trend toward extraconstitutional behavior emanating from the White House, along with a divided and often-enfeebled Congress, may have grown weary of the expression "our institutions will hold" in recent years. Yet the hope that the American judicial system would stay the hand of the mob, or the president for that matter—a conflated reality, to be sure, given the insurrection on the nation's Capitol on January 6, 2021—became a sort of palliative for dark and uncertain times.

Aside from this one mention of the legislative branch, and Lincoln's reference to George Washington, the only attention to America's political institutions is given to the courts, and these are small nods at that. Like Alexis de Tocqueville, Lincoln believes Americans need to return to building what Tocqueville called the "habits of the heart" with respect to democracy. Education, both political and moral, is to be the way forward for a citizenry that is further and further removed from the founding generation. As Tocqueville expressed it in *Democracy in America*, published three years before the Lyceum Address,

> I understand here the expression *moeurs* in the sense the ancients attached to the word mores; not only do I apply to mores properly so-called, which one could call habits of the heart, but to the different notions that men possess, to the various opinions that are current in their midst, and to the sum of ideas of which the habits of the mind are formed. . . . My goal is not to make a picture of American mores; I limit myself at this moment to searching among them for what is favorable to the maintenance of political institutions.[40]

This similarity in language between Lincoln (perpetuation) and Tocqueville (maintenance) on the subject of promulgating America's political institutions emanates from the belief that democracy is more than the sum of the powers explicitly provided to its institutions. On the contrary, democracy is only as strong as its people, and it is their principled and moral grounding that creates an almost instinctive adherence to the requisites of self-government. Madison has it backward: A dependence on the *people*, rather than political institutions, must be the primary control on the government. People needn't be angels to successfully administer self-government; but they must habituate themselves to moral, if not angelic, political behavior.

This brings us to Lincoln's use of the word "habits" at the Lyceum. Speaking of the "outrages committed by mobs," Lincoln says "they spring up among the pleasure-hunting masters of Southern slaves, and the order-loving citizens of the land of steady habits.—Whatever, then, their cause may be, it is common to the whole country." If ever there was a subtle rebuke of slavery, this is it. From the beginning of his address, Lincoln argues that mob violence is not strictly a Southern phenomenon, but rather a national one. On the surface, it seems that Lincoln is once again showing his moderate face—a kind of "both sides-ism." Yet, Lincoln's use of the expression "the land of steady habits" to describe the free states is a direct criticism of slavery. People with steady habits do their own work; those who lack them force others to do it.

It is important to note that "the pleasure-hunting masters of Southern slaves" are contrasted with "order-loving" citizens who are not slave owners. The latter are the practitioners of the steady habits of democracy. That they too are susceptible to mob violence suggests that Lincoln sees the problem of lawlessness as universal; but "order-loving" and "pleasure-hunting" people are not moral equals. This is a condemnation of slavery without explicitly saying so. The formulation suggests that slavery weakens the adherence to the rule of law, even if it is, at times, violated in states where slavery does not exist. The land of steady habits is better equipped for democratic life, though it is not immune to being party to assaults upon it. And if there is a thread connecting the three cases Lincoln invokes in his address, it is that of slavery and race in America.

• • •

NOT ONLY DOES LINCOLN INCLUDE CASES CONNECTED TO race and slavery in his examples of mob violence in the recent past, he describes them as "the most dangerous" and "revolting to humanity." These are the Mississippi lynchings that include the gamblers, enslaved African Americans, and whites "leagued with Negroes," along with the burning of Francis McIntosh. Lincoln's recounting of Lovejoy's shooting does not include similarly pejorative adjectives, though Lovejoy's murderers are described as "vicious."[41] Lincoln says it would be "tedious as well as useless to recount the horrors," out of the universe of recent cases—so he singles out the most horrific of the lot. If Lincoln wanted to tread lightly around the subject of slavery or race, he had, as mentioned, any number of incidents around the country against "innocent" whites to select from.

"What [do these murders have] to do with the perpetuation of our political institutions?" Lincoln asks. In short, he argues that American democracy is only as strong as our willingness to protect the rights of those we hold in low regard. The gamblers "constitute a portion of population that is worse than useless in any community," Lincoln says. Similarly, McIntosh "had forfeited his life, by the perpetration of an outrageous murder, upon one of the most worthy and respectable citizens [Dr. Bodley] of the city."[42] But Lincoln points out that gambling was permitted by Mississippi's legislature, and that McIntosh would have in all probability faced the death penalty upon a lawful conviction. If we are to acknowledge these views as examples of Lincoln's "moderate" disposition because he is no fan of gamblers nor of murder, then we are also bound to recognize his willingness to defend those held in disdain by many Illinoisians whose votes he was desirous of attaining.

In a sense, this is an act of faith on the part of Lincoln. He chooses to believe that the deeper appreciation for the rule of law, of respect for due process among his audience, is greater than any particular hatred or fear. The logical progression for Lincoln is that "the mob of to-morrow, may, and probably will, hang or burn [the innocent] by the very same mistake."[43] This is related to Alexis de Tocqueville's idea of self-interest, *bien entendu*, or properly understood.[44] Injustice anywhere is a threat to justice everywhere, as Martin Luther King Jr. expressed it. If this is Lincoln attempting to stake out a safe political position, he is in good company. Full legal protection for the marginalized is the basis for any system of government seeking to rise above the baser instincts or passions among human beings. In a sense, Lincoln believes we are failing Hamilton's first question concerning the nature of America's political experiment, as articulated in the very first Federalist:

> [W]hether societies of men are really capable or not of establishing good government from reflection and choice, or whether they are forever destined to depend for their political constitutions on accident and force.[45]

If Lincoln departs some ways from Hamilton in his greater faith in the people, he hews closely to his view that self-government is very much related to the feelings citizens have for their government. "Thus, then, by the operation of this mobocratic spirit," Lincoln says, "which all must admit, is now abroad in the land, the strongest bulwark of any Government, and particularly of those constituted like ours, may effectually be broken down and destroyed—I mean the *attachment* of the People."[46]

This word, "attachment," carried a stronger meaning in the early American republic than we give it today with respect to politics. It is a word that appears frequently in the *Federalist Papers* and has a strong presence in Washington's Farewell Address. Lincoln believes the tenuousness of the people's attachment to their government threatens "the fondest hope, of the lovers of freedom, throughout the world."[47] If this language sounds familiar, it is because Lincoln will say something close to it in his December 1, 1862, Message to Congress, when he said, "In giving freedom to the slave, we assure freedom to the free—honorable alike in what we give, and what we preserve. We shall nobly save, or meanly lose, the last best hope of earth."[48]

The *fondest* hope, the *best* hope, is a government ruled by the people themselves—and this hope can only be made possible by giving full rights—in a word, freedom—to the least among us. Two months after he announced the Emancipation Proclamation, Lincoln was not articulating the philosophy of a man "forced into glory"; he was a man returning to his first principles.[49] The Lyceum Address presages the connections Lincoln will more famously and significantly make as president, between racial justice and emancipation, and the quality of American democracy.

If Lincoln is conservative in his Lyceum address, it is because he is no anarchist. The role of government may be a necessary one as Madison articulated in Federalist 10. "If men were angels, no government would be necessary," Madison famously wrote. Speaking fifty years after the publication of the *Federalist Papers* at the Lyceum, Lincoln surveyed the ill-effects of government's absence. "Having ever regarded Government as their deadliest bane," Lincoln said, "[mobs] make a jubilee of the suspension of its operations; and pray for nothing so much, as its total annihilation."[50]

We cannot love government only in proportion to its ability to support and defend those we identify with. That it is charged with protecting *gamblers*, *Negroes*, and *those leagued with Negroes*, cannot be cause to abandon it. Such a view calls to mind Ronald Reagan's often-quoted line from his First Inaugural Address, "Government is not the answer to our problems, government *is* the problem."[51] This was a view whose popularity was in part owed to a broad perception among many whites that the government had spent too many resources over too many years aiding and supporting African Americans and other groups. That Lincoln emphasized that the inevitable consequence of this dim view of government would be a general lawlessness that would ultimately assault the very people who espouse it doesn't diminish the significance of his staking the claim on the basis of fundamental equality among all Americans. A selective reverence and respect for the government is not only morally wrong, it is, to use Lincoln's word, suicidal.

It is a critical feature of the Lyceum Address that Lincoln closes by returning to George Washington and the legacy of the founders. Notably, Washington's Farewell Address warned against similar dangers to national unity. But Lincoln's speech advances the Farewell's message considerably. Washington's unity was premised upon shared social and cultural characteristics. "With slight shades of difference, you have the same religion, manners, habits, and political principles," Washington said in his message. "You have in a common cause fought and triumphed together. The independence and liberty you possess are the work of joint councils and joint efforts—of common dangers, sufferings, and successes."[52] But what about those whose religion, manners, habits, principles—and it must be said though it remains unspoken by Washington—*race* are different? What then? Lincoln's Lyceum Address is the first and best answer to this question, and among its many admirable and overlooked traits, it also serves as an invaluable coda to Washington's greatest political message.

WHERE THE FIRST HALF OF THE LYCEUM ADDRESS IS devoted to describing the nature and causes of America's slide toward lawlessness, the second half begins the process of addressing Lincoln's query, "How shall we fortify against it?" Lincoln's answer isn't a call for more legislation—there is no cry for tougher laws against vigilantism. This is because Lincoln sees the rise of antidemocratic behavior as fundamentally a spiritual problem. Something has changed in the character of the nation, and it can only be addressed by reshaping who we are as a people. Lincoln's remedy begins with an oath, and it is worth quoting at length:

> The answer is simple. Let every American, every lover of liberty, every well wisher to his posterity, swear by the blood of the Revolution, never to violate in the least particular, the laws of the country; and never to tolerate their violation by others. As the patriots of seventy-six did to the support of the Declaration of Independence,

> so to the support of the Constitution and Laws. Let every American pledge his life, his property, and his sacred honor; —let every man remember that to violate the law, is to trample on the blood of his father, and to tear the character of his own, and his children's liberty. Let reverence for the laws, be breathed by every American mother, to the lisping babe, that prattles on her lap—let it be taught in school, in seminaries, and in colleges; let it be written in Primers, spelling books, and in Almanacs;—let it be preached from the pulpit, proclaimed in legislative halls, and enforced in courts of justice. And, in short, let it become the *political religion* of the nation; and let the old and the young, the rich and the poor, the grave and the gay, of all sexes and tongues, and colors and conditions, sacrifice unceasingly upon its altars.[53]

If Madison is correct that the "latent cause of faction are . . . sown in the nature of man," Lincoln's solution isn't to rework a Constitution that already takes that into account, dividing and separating powers, and so forth.[54] Democracy is very much a feeling, a point I will explore further shortly. As such, it is only as strong and good as the promises one makes to oneself. Lincoln's Lyceum, like Jefferson's Declaration, believes in pledges and oaths. It is a rhetorical device he will return to at Gettysburg ("*we here highly resolve that these dead shall not have died in vain*") and in the Second Inaugural ("*with malice toward none with charity for all*"). These latter two are unnamed oaths, but oaths they are. They are promises one makes to oneself and to the nation—hence undergirding the "political religion" Lincoln calls for.

Beyond an oath, Lincoln calls for a lifelong education in the values of democracy, none greater than "reverence for the laws." This secularizes the kind of religious education William Stewart was extolling. On a different front with respect to education, the lone reference to women in the Lyceum Address is the call for mothers to instruct their infants in this attachment to the laws; it is an extension of what scholars have referred to as "republican motherhood"—the education in civic republicanism thought to be the responsibility of mothers in the early republic.[55] It is an unmistakably confining and patriarchal vestige of the period lauded by Lincoln. If a saving grace is to be had in its resurrection by him, it is to be found in the virtues of democracy itself, a principle whose power cannot be confined, as he says, "to [the] old [or] the young, the rich [or] the poor, the grave [or] the gay." It is, he says, for "all sexes and tongues, and colors and conditions." These latter couplings complement the Lincoln who supported women's suffrage in his campaign announcement of 1836 and who opposed slavery in his statement to the Illinois legislature in 1837.

Lincoln's reverence for the laws does not, however, abide the philosophy of a Henry David Thoreau or Martin Luther King Jr., who supported the defiance of unjust and unnatural laws. But Thoreau and King also advocated a willingness to face the legal consequences for violating them. This is a different kind of defiance than that of the radical abolitionist John Brown or, more familiar to our time, of Eric Snowden. In a sense, the former remains attached to the law, by dint of their willingness to go to jail for violating it. This is truly Socratic in its example. Still, this goes too far for Lincoln, who says, "Let me not be understood as saying there are no bad laws, nor that grievances may not arise, for the redress of which, no legal provisions have been made.—I mean to say no such thing. But I do mean to say, that, although bad laws, if they exist, should be repealed as soon as possible, still while they continue in force, for the sake of example, they should be religiously observed."[56] Lincoln is not worried about a Thoreau or a King willfully going to jail for passively resisting an unjust law; he's instead worried about the mob's violence in defiance of the rule of law. It is a subtle but important distinction underlying his argument at the Lyceum. Nonviolent civil disobedience is a far cry from the murderous scenes described by Lincoln at Vicksburg, St. Louis, and Alton.

If a descent into anarchy is Lincoln's chief worry, then its secondary effect is the prospect of an ambitious, talented, and unscrupulous leader rising to power, whose only motive is self-empowerment. In Lincoln's own time, Andrew Jackson was perceived as an obsessively self-interested and overbearing executive, one bordering on the behavior of a monarch rather than a republican executive. Some scholars have suggested Jackson as the unspoken "towering genius" Lincoln references in his speech, while others have made the case it was more likely a reference to Jackson's successor, Martin Van Buren.[57] Here is Lincoln's line in question:

> Towering genius disdains a beaten path. It seeks regions hitherto unexplored.—It sees *no distinction* in adding story to story, upon the monuments of fame, erected to the memory of others. It *denies* that it is glory enough to serve under any chief. It *scorns* to tread in the footsteps of *any* predecessor, however illustrious.[58]

The reference to a predecessor is a giveaway to some, that it's Van Buren on Lincoln's mind. But it is just as likely—and I argue more likely—that it's the founders on Lincoln's mind, those "fathers" he crafts the entirety of his speech around. The "successor" is unknown, lurking about or unborn. But, for Lincoln, the conditions are there to produce, "at some time," an American "Alexander, Caesar, or Napoleon."[59]

Historian Douglass Adair made the subject of fame a more central focus for modern scholars for understanding the type of distinction valued by the revolutionary generation. Adair's 1974 book, *Fame and the Founding Fathers*, published posthumously, emphasized the republican ideals of the founders, particularly his essay of the same title, which placed their ambitions in the context of their time.[60] This is very much what Lincoln does at the Lyceum, seeing in the "fathers" a healthy desire for fame, because, in their time, "all that sought celebrity and fame, and distinction, expected to find them in the success of that experiment. Their *all* was staked upon it:—their destiny was *inseparably* linked with it. Their ambition aspired to display before an admiring world, a practical demonstration of the truth of a proposition, which had hitherto been considered, at best no better, than problematical; namely, *the capability of a people to govern themselves*."[61] In short, heroism in the early republic was linked to its success.

Lincoln worries that this is no longer the case because the "field of glory has been harvested." The founding generation and its "living history," as he put it, is no more.[62] Critics of Lincoln's ornate and flowery language at the Lyceum undoubtedly don't care for allusions to the founders as a "forest of giant oaks" or the passage of that generation to "mutilated limbs," but romanticism and its excesses aside, it's Lincoln's point that matters. Democracy is a feeling that must be conveyed, and it is done by example, through storytelling and persistent education.

This brings us to writer Charles Baxter's 2017 lecture, delivered the summer after Donald Trump's inauguration in Vermont at the Bread Loaf Writers' Conference. In a highly engaging and deeply moving lecture, Baxter explored the loss of democracy as a gradual phenomenon—in the category of "Things About to Disappear," the title of his talk. Such things include veiled hats worn by women, to more recent disappearances such as saying, "You're welcome," in exchange for the more informal and graceless "No problem." But the most poignant example from Baxter's talk, one given so writers might be better curators of their world (and democratic citizens of their politics) was the story of French composer Manuel Rosenthal trying, in the 1980s, to get his class of Juilliard Symphony Orchestra musicians to play an old number that he cherished from his youth, created by his mentor Maurice Ravel. Try as he might, they simply couldn't get the feeling of the song right, even as they played the correct notes. Finally, as Baxter related the story, Rosenthal relented. "No, it is gone," he said.[63] No one alive today was alive when the feeling of that song was born, and no one today could replicate it. As Lincoln put it at the Lyceum, "This state of feeling *must fade, is fading, has faded*, with the circumstances that produced it."

IF THERE IS A SPIRIT LINCOLN WANTS TO RESURRECT, IT IS the spirit that yearns for democratic distinction. Lincoln historians and psychobiographers have wondered about Lincoln subliminally, or otherwise, placing himself in the role of democracy's savior. An oft chewed-on line is the one where Lincoln notes that towering genius "thirsts and burns for distinction; and, if possible, it will have it, whether at the expense of emancipating slaves, or enslaving freemen."[64] It is admittedly hard, if not impossible, not to consider this line in the context of Lincoln's unique role in ending slavery in America. The other line is Lincoln's mysterious conjuring of George Washington at the close of his address.

> Passion has helped us; but can do so no more. It will in future be our enemy. Reason, cold, calculating, unimpassioned reason, must furnish all the materials for our future support and defence.—Let those materials be moulded into *general intelligence, sound morality*, and in particular, *a reverence for the constitution and laws*: and, that we improved to the last; that we remained free to the last; that we revered his name to the last; that, during his long sleep, we permitted no hostile foot to pass over or desecrate his resting place; shall be that which to learn the last trump shall awaken our WASHINGTON.

It is a verbose and complicated ending—"shall be that which to learn" is painfully awkward wording. But if we move the conversation to Lincoln's intentions, we are back to Washington as a metaphor for something greater than the antidemocratic figures he references in his speech. Washington's heroism is that of the dutiful republican, the heroism of restraint. Walking away from power is incredibly difficult; walking away from power when experienced at its height, perhaps impossible. Yet Washington's gesture gifted a spirit of democratic virtue that lasted from 1796 to 1940, until Franklin D. Roosevelt ran for a third term.

Washington's is a fading example, whether in the more benign case of Michael Bloomberg orchestrating a third term as mayor of New York in 2009, or Donald Trump far more nefariously attempting to orchestrate an insurrection to overturn the election of 2020. A democracy can only experience the "unprecedented" for so long before a generation comes to experience it as routine. Before Kamala Harris's recent address, my undergraduate students could scarcely remember a concession speech after a presidential election—and for good reason. The last one they witnessed, if at all, came when they were twelve or thirteen. It is not hard to imagine another four years, or more, before seeing another. Concession speeches at all levels now appear to be newsworthy events.

For all of Lincoln's talk of reason at the Lyceum, his primary objective was to retain an underlying passion for self-government and the rule of law. Democratic life is a romantic venture, and all of the small accoutrements of love are necessary for its sustenance. We may perform the rites and rituals guided by reason, but we sustain them over the long haul out of love. Lincoln's last line, after all, is passionate one—a metaphorical call to arms from scripture, taken from this passage in the Book of Matthew:

> And I say also unto thee, That thou art Peter, and upon this rock I will build my church; and the gates of hell shall not prevail against it.[65]

For Lincoln, self-government is indeed the great hope of the world. It is the civil heaven of his civil religion, as Washington is that religion's Peter.

> Upon these let the proud fabric of freedom rest, as the rock of its basis; and as truly as has been said of the only greater institution, "*the gates of hell shall not prevail against it.*"[66]

True to his prophetic form, Lincoln ends his address by calling to mind something greater than ourselves.

• • •

"IT WAS HIGHLY SOPHOMORIC IN CHARACTER AND ABOUNDED in striking and lofty metaphor," Lincoln's law partner William Herndon would write of the Lyceum Address in 1888. Yet Herndon concluded, "In point of rhetorical effort it excels anything he ever afterward attempted."[67] Most Lincoln scholars would agree with the former statement; few, if any, would subscribe to the latter. The Lyceum Address, for all of its virtues, does not belong in the same class as the Gettysburg Address, nor should it be compared to the Second Inaugural, Lincoln's most radical speech. Except in one regard. Like the Second Inaugural, it has a dark and prophetic tone that implicates America's political sins in the nation's present troubles. Taken with the House Divided Speech of 1858, the Lyceum is the first epistle in a dark trilogy of warnings for the United States delivered over twenty-seven years (1838–1865). The critical lines linking the speeches are as follows:

> "As a nation of freemen, we must live through all time, or die by suicide."
>
> "A house divided against itself cannot stand."
>
> "Yet, if God wills that [the Civil War] continue until all the wealth piled by the bondsman's two hundred and fifty years of unrequited toil shall be sunk and until

> every drop of blood drawn with the lash shall be paid by another drawn with the sword as was said three thousand years ago so still it must be said 'the judgments of the Lord are true and righteous altogether.'"

Lincoln returns to the Book of Matthew in his House Divided Speech, delivered at the Illinois Republican State Convention in Springfield on June 16, 1858. Here is the scripture:

> Every kingdom divided against itself is brought to desolation, and every city or house divided against itself will not stand. If Satan casts out Satan, he is divided against himself. How then will his kingdom stand? (Matthew 12:25–26, KJV)

When Lincoln says, "I do not expect the house to *fall,*" he is arguing that the United States will either persist as an entirely free nation, or one where slavery is legal everywhere. But the underlying argument is that slavery is the evil to be cast out, just as Jesus is refuting his critics for his casting out demons—something another demon would not do. In short, the source of the division is a moral one. Slavery and freedom are no more equal than the demons cast out by Christ are His equal. Southerners were not needlessly fretting over Lincoln's clear antagonism toward slavery—and they were proven right when Lincoln ultimately issued the Emancipation Proclamation. His demurring over the question in his First Inaugural belied the strength of his earlier antislavery statements, including his low regard for the "pleasure-hunting masters of Southern slaves" he references in his Lyceum Address.

Lincoln's 1858 address prophesies what is to come. "In *my* opinion," he says concerning antislavery agitation, "it *will* not cease, until a *crisis* shall have been reached, and passed."[68] In this first speech upon accepting the Republican Party nomination for senator, Lincoln sees an inevitable reckoning with a divided America whose division is not simply political but deeply moral.

In his Second Inaugural, Lincoln's scriptural reference is pulled from the Old Testament, found in the Nineteenth Psalm.

> The fear of the LORD is clean, enduring for ever: The judgments of the LORD are true and righteous altogether. (Psalms 19: 9–10)

Here, the Lyceum's warning of national suicide has played out over the course of four years of war and the loss of some 750,000 lives. The dark prophecy has come to pass, with Lincoln imploring the nation to accept the divine wrath it has earned. It is the pathway to the healing balm of his speech's concluding line, beginning with: "With malice toward none with charity for all." The absence of malice is an important first step, but it is not the equal of *caritas*—the deep love, implicit in the words and deeds of charity.

A careful reading of these three speeches reveals that, for Lincoln, freedom is the pathway to national salvation. Only "a nation of freemen" can escape "suicide," he tells us in 1838 at the Lyceum. In 1858, he said, "I believe this government cannot endure permanently half slave and half free." Freedom was the hinge upon which the nature of national unity was to be determined. And when this question could only be answered through war, Lincoln's Second Inaugural's grim algebraic equation called for the "bondsman's two hundred and fifty years of unrequited toil" to be paid for in blood and treasure. If Americans have too often casually tossed about the term "freedom" to define the essence of their country's identity, Lincoln reminded them that that freedom must be universal or nothing at all. Selective freedom leads to "nihilism and chaos" (the Lyceum Address), "division and crisis" (the House Divided speech), and ultimately, "suffering and death" (the Second Inaugural).

The Lyceum Address is not Abraham Lincoln's greatest speech, nor is it the one that made him president or changed America, as others have suggested defined his most famous speeches.[69] But the Lyceum Address is the Rosetta stone to Lincoln's political thought. It is the speech that links all that follow. Most importantly, it is the source of those virtues to be found in his greatest acts—compassion for the weak, justice for the marginalized, and hope for the afflicted. And it has the virtue of being first not only in chronology, but in generating the field of thought from which all else was cultivated.

FIVE

FORTIFICATIONS

Abraham Lincoln would live another twenty-three years in Springfield, Illinois, before departing for Washington on February 11, 1861, to become the nation's sixteenth president. "I now leave," he told the crowd gathered at the local train depot, "not knowing when, or whether ever, I may return, with a task before me greater than that which rested upon Washington."[1] His body would return to Springfield on May 3, 1865, aboard a funeral train that had traveled over 1,600 miles, carrying him and his son William, who had died in the White House at age eleven in February of 1862. As the nation's first president to be assassinated, Lincoln's death ushered in a period of unparalleled mourning. Shot on Good Friday, and dying the next morning, he became the Christ-like figure in the civil religion he spoke of in his Lyceum Address. As *The New York Times* reported on the arrival of his body back home:

> The tears which are shed while glancing at the shrinking features of the deceased, attest the depth of the

> grief which affects the hearts of those who were well acquainted with their martyr citizen.[2]

Fittingly, the Lincoln Memorial remains the altar for national public gatherings seeking redress for political change.

Over the course of those remaining years in Springfield, Lincoln was reelected to the General Assembly of the Illinois legislature in 1838 and 1840, argued a case before the Illinois State Supreme Court, went into private law practice with William Herndon, and most notably, was elected to the House of Representatives in 1846, serving but one term—the highest elective office he would hold until becoming president in March of 1861. His public speeches and letters, along with his debates with Stephen Douglas, would become important parts of a pre-presidential record that has deepened America's and, indeed, the world's understanding of Lincoln as both a man and a political figure. The thirst for information, however small or seemingly insignificant, about Lincoln remains unquenchable.

And yet there have been no books about the "martyr citizen's" first significant public address. In fairness, the "Young Men's Lyceum" as a forum sounds stale and unfashionably masculine, if not dull. "The Perpetuation of Our Political Institutions" as a title for a public address likewise does not inspire in an age of catchphrases and well-selected sound bites. Given what his leadership skills would ultimately be called to respond to, there seemed to be very little at stake for Lincoln in 1838—there was no great war, no significant office up for grabs, no counterpunching rival to best. It was simply a young, aspiring politician giving a talk at a local club in the middle of winter in a small Midwestern town.

But as I hope appears to be clear by now, the Lyceum Address is no mere footnote to Lincoln's career. It was a speech filled with genuine political courage, one that reveals the political DNA that Lincoln would carry with him for the rest of his life. It reflects his great passions: the advancement of self-government; the rule of law; and a political equality antithetical to racism and slavery. This is the nature of the "union" Lincoln was desirous of upholding. We know this because the Lincoln who finally emerges is not the Lincoln arguing that he would "save the Union without freeing any slave," if he could do it. That's more in keeping with the logic of his 1864 presidential opponent George B. McClellan, who had pledged to do just that.[3] No—Lincoln the "Emancipator" is the person who, at the very beginning, sought justice for the dregs of American society in the age of Jackson: the gamblers, the Francis McIntoshes, and the Elijah P. Lovejoys—those whom most of his white contemporaries found sufficient reason to hang, burn, and shoot, or looked the other way, with little shame or remorse.

Over the decades, the Lyceum Address has made numerous appearances in America's political fights. Nobody argues over the meaning of Gettysburg, for example—not seriously, anyway. That's like arguing with the "Sermon on the Mount." But the Lyceum has become worth fighting over because it is the earliest, most comprehensive window into Lincoln's political thought. And it contains enough ambiguity, certainly for casual readers, to claim versions of Lincoln that suit their politics. As such, it has had a most intriguing history in the life of the nation, with its admirers comprising an assortment of odd political bedfellows.

JUST OVER A MONTH BEFORE THE PRESIDENTIAL ELECTION of 1912—and eleven days before he was to survive an assassination attempt—Theodore Roosevelt was the subject of a letter to the editor of *The New York Times*. The letter, likely the first reference to Lincoln's Lyceum Address in the *Times*, is highly representative of how the speech has been used by its readers over time to defend or attack any variety of ideological positions. "Mr. Roosevelt has been saying very much of late about his intellectual descent from Lincoln," the unnamed writer began. "Has he read the martyr President's warning against ambitious demagogues: Genius disdains a beaten path. It scorns to tread in the footstep of any predecessor. It thirsts and burns for distinction, and if possible it will have it, whether at the expense of emancipating slaves or enslaving freemen." The *Times* letter then goes on to quote from the Lyceum at length before closing.[4]

As Nathaniel Philbrick has written about Herman Melville's Captain Ahab, the Lyceum Address's unnamed tyrant has likewise served as a generational reminder about the looming dangers of tyrannical power. While Donald Trump has been the most recent example of this concern, as the above letter shows, he has hardly been the first president to have had this comparison made with him in mind. "It is why subsequent generations have seen Ahab as Hitler during World War II or as a profit-crazed deep-drilling oil company in 2010 or as a power-crazed Middle Eastern dictator in 2011," Philbrick has written.[5] Lincoln's anonymous "towering genius" of the Lyceum and Melville's Ahab are cut from the same cloth that fears lurking authoritarianism.

If Theodore Roosevelt was a symbol of internal menace for some during the Progressive Era, it was domestic communists of the Cold War era who came to represent an internal threat to American democracy. In his 1950 Lincoln's Day Address in which he claimed to have a list of known communists within the State Department, Senator Joseph McCarthy crudely paraphrased the Lyceum Address. "As one of our outstanding historical figures once said, 'When a great democracy is destroyed, it will not be because of enemies from without but rather because of enemies from within," McCarthy said.[6] This mangling of the "die by suicide" line from the Lyceum has been so frequently abused that, in 2021, Reuters corralled a number of Lincoln historians to refute the "enemies from within" misquote attributed to Lincoln.[7]

However well or poorly understood, the Lyceum's unsettling theme of internal decay has resonated over the years. As historian Jason H. Silverman has written,

> Readers of Lincoln have exploited quotations from the Lyceum Address to justify myriad situations. The law-and-order passages have had a particularly long shelf life. For instance, in 1915, Outlook quoted Lincoln's warnings about mob rule to condemn the lynching of a Jewish manager in Atlanta. Then in 1948, Lincoln's "reverence for the laws" passages were used quite differently and ironically when famed liberal United States Senator Wayne Morse of Oregon advised labor leader A. Philip Randolph not to take up civil disobedience in response to segregation. Similarly, in 1966, Chicago Mayor Richard J. Daley quoted Lincoln on "reverence for the laws" in an effort to quell civil rights protestors.[8]

The tendency to read the Lyceum Address one way, mirrors similarly rigid views of Lincoln. Political scientist Brian Danoff has said it well, reminding us "that Lincoln's goal was not simply to ensure the mere physical survival of the Union. Instead, Lincoln wanted to save the state on the basis of certain principles—to be precise, the principles that he thought were embodied in the Revolution and the Declaration of Independence."[9] This subtle but important caveat compels more attentiveness to both the content and context of Lincoln's words. While not always the case, the tendency to read the Lyceum Address narrowly often suggests more about the reader's politics than Lincoln's.

As John Channing Briggs has put it, "For Lincoln, of course, the problem of perpetuating self-government was connected, from the earliest stages of his career, with the anomaly of slavery's presence in a self-governing republic."[10] For too long, and for too many, it has been one or the other, but mostly the former. This interpretive tendency has made the "law and order" (a phrase Lincoln does not use) reading of the Lyceum far weightier than warranted.

Admittedly, it is hard to resist the allure of the Lyceum's pull to see all manner of America's ills as a pathway to national suicide. Overly wary of the growing military industrial complex of the late 1950s, James Reston of *The New York Times* called the Lyceum Address in as his expert witness to highlight the growing need to finance more domestic programs, including Congress's need to "set a standard for high school graduation."[11] What problem *can't* the Lyceum Address solve? The speech's catch-all invitation has been its great power—but also part of its undoing. That's because the specificity of Lincoln's message against mob violence—and every example he provides is profoundly tied to race—has been historically unpleasant, or not in keeping with the conventional wisdom that Lincoln was only tangentially interested in race.

The highly influential political theorist Harry V. Jaffa may have been among the first scholars to describe the Lyceum Address as prophetic. His view was informed by historian Edmund Wilson's conclusion that the Lyceum was, indeed, a "startlingly prophetic" utterance of Lincoln.[12] In his classic 1959 work, *Crisis of the House Divided*, Jaffa compared the *prophesying* Lyceum Address to the *proclaiming* Gettysburg Address.[13] He went on to write of "Lincoln's prophetic account of the coming crisis" in the Lyceum as necessitating a refounding of America that takes into account the ever-present possibility that ambitious leaders may seek to usurp the democratic enterprise.

> Thus we see that, for the republic to live, the act of creation or founding must be repeated. Indeed, we may go further and say that Lincoln's argument carried to its logical conclusion requires that the re-creation of the republic is something that may have to be accomplished at any time and that only as there are men of transcendent ability and virtue who, in the sense indicated, stand guard outside the community can those within it remain in possession of their republican rights.[14]

In this probing essay, Jaffa sees Lincoln's opposition to gambling and slavery in the Lyceum as moral wrongs that nevertheless as "sanctioned by law" should not be overturned violently. But this goes too far in suggesting a moral equivalency on the matter for Lincoln. The better comparison might be between Lincoln's views of gambling and alcoholism, which Lincoln believed to be personal moral failings that should not inspire violence. Slavery, on the other hand for Lincoln, is a personal, as well as *political*, moral failing. Lincoln's implicit condemnation of "the pleasure-hunting masters of Southern slaves" in the Lyceum suggests as much. But Jaffa views this explicit reference to slavery as only suggestive, not dispositive, of Lincoln's moral judgment against these racially motivated acts of mob violence. "Lincoln minimized the intrinsic evil of hanging gamblers and burning murderers without due process of law," Jaffa writes.[15] Jaffa's essay on the Lyceum is compelling in many ways—but nothing could be further from the truth. We know this because Lincoln's contemporaries who delivered Lyceum Addresses around the same time and covered the same themes didn't bother to mention the gamblers or McIntosh at all. Now *that's* minimizing evil.

Jaffa's skepticism about Lincoln's moral absolutism on the question of slavery or racial injustice has to contend with something like the great philosophical quandary: *Why does the universe exist at all?* The same can be said for the presence of McIntosh and the lynched Blacks of Mississippi in the Lyceum Address—not to mention the highly controversial Lovejoy. Wouldn't it have been prudent of Lincoln to make his "due process" and anti-mob case without them if he truly wanted to "minimize" their deaths? Jaffa's view holds only if Lincoln did not believe deeply that slavery and racial hatreds were intertwined with the very character of the antidemocratic trends he saw growing in his time. Lincoln's Lyceum Address is darkly prophetic in large part because it underscores the price the United States will pay for its inability to contend with passions emanating from racial animus as much as the passions embodied by an unseen Caesar.

"If it took courage in the Springfield of 1838 to express sympathy for an abolitionist like Lovejoy," Lincoln biographer Michael Burlingame has written, "it required even more nerve to speak compassionately of a black man who in April 1836 had stabbed two white men."[16] Burlingame is right about Lincoln's use of Francis McIntosh in the Lyceum Address. Had he wished, Lincoln could have just as easily invoked McIntosh as an example of those responsible for the rise of lawlessness throughout the land, instead of choosing to center him as one of its victims.

• • •

ACCORDING TO GOOGLE NGRAM, WHICH TRACKS SUCH things, the term "lyceum speech" has been rising over the past decade and is now in as much use as it had been in 1964. It appears during periods of great social turmoil and division—the 1930s, 1960s, 1990s, and today—evidence upward spikes in attentiveness to the Lyceum Address.[17] But this is closer to guesswork than hard science. Still, if you're noticing the speech's presence in public discourse more, you're not wrong. Its resurgence clearly has much to do with the political rise and presidency—and now, reelection—of Donald Trump. And it certainly has to do with the increasing prevalence of high-profile acts of mob violence—including the extrajudicial shooting of unarmed African Americans by members of law enforcement. But how successful at "fortifying"—to borrow Lincoln's word—has our democratic system been against mob violence in the decades before Trump's political emergence? And what are the lessons we should take from the Lyceum today, given the prescriptions Lincoln laid out for Americans back in 1838?

To be sure, the decades after the Lyceum Address confirmed Lincoln's worst fears. From the nativist violence of the Know-Nothings, to the small-scale and confined civil war that became known as "Bleeding Kansas"—along with the ever-present phenomenon of lynchings—the mid-nineteenth century was in many ways defined by mob violence.[18] Most ironically, Lincoln would be assassinated as a race traitor in his own right, according to the warped mind of John Wilkes Booth, whose inspiration for killing the president was Lincoln's suggestion of Black voting rights on the horizon. "That means nigger citizenship," Boot is purported to have said. "That is the last speech he will ever make."[19]

As we know, any prospects for a return to a reverence for the laws after the Civil War faltered in the aftermath of Reconstruction. While precise numbers can never truly be learned, an Equal Justice Initiative study estimates that there were "more than 2,000 Black victims killed during the Reconstruction era, from 1865 to 1876," and "more than 4,400 victims documented for the seventy-four-year era of racial lynching terror that spans 1877 to 1950."[20] The photographic record of American lynchings in the twentieth century only accentuates Lincoln's Lyceum account of the Mississippi murders of 1835, where "dead men were seen literally dangling from the boughs of trees upon every road side; and in numbers almost sufficient, to rival the native Spanish moss of the country, as a drapery of the forest."[21]

What the numbers don't account for is the terror that Black families lived through during this period, a fear that may no longer be quite as intense but has hardly dissipated entirely. And, of course, mob violence also greatly afflicted immigrant communities in America, especially Chinese immigrants, as well as Catholic and southern European communities. The marginalization of Jews from much of early twentieth-century American social and political institutions was also accompanied by episodic violence. The role of extrajudicial violence against marginalized communities, from Muslims (MENA) to queer Americans, likewise remains a part of everyday American life. This is not to mention the terror of random violence from mass shootings that provide the hum of low-grade terror, simply from visiting a shopping mall, attending a religious service, or enjoying a musical performance. In sum, there has never been a time where the Lyceum Address's warnings were outdated, or Lincoln's prescience easily dismissed. Americans live in the young Lincoln's nightmare, with no end in sight.

What's different now is that a segment of the official political class has embraced the mob. Perhaps the greatest vanishing act out of Charles Baxter's "things about to disappear" is the formerly unbroken line of nonviolent transfers of powers occasioned by presidential elections. The insurrection at the Capitol on January 6, 2021, seeking to interrupt the constitutionally mandated counting of electoral votes, led to 7 deaths, 150 Capitol and Metropolitan Police injured, and scores traumatized by the event.[22] It may be impossible to know the damage caused to the national psyche with respect to America's collective confidence in the political process, one that had already been weakened in recent decades. A generation of citizens that witnessed intelligence and policy failures from 9/11 to the war in Iraq, to Hurricane Katrina, to the Great Recession, to the coronavirus pandemic, has now had added to the list a failed coup that nearly led to the assassination of the vice president and speaker of the House. Lincoln may have fathomed a Caesar or Napoleon attempting to pull down the temple of American democracy; what he did not prophesy was that the "mobocratic spirit" would penetrate one of America's great political parties—indeed, the party he helped to establish. It turns out that Lincoln may have failed to imagine just how far the polity could yield to what he called "the basest principles of our nature."[23]

As the shooting of Elijah P. Lovejoy was preceded by the burning of Francis McIntosh and the hangings of gamblers in Mississippi, the mob violence at the Capitol was preceded by other deeply worrisome extrajudicial killings. On May 25, 2020, a forty-six-year-old African American man named George Floyd was murdered in police custody in Minneapolis after allegedly purchasing cigarettes with a counterfeit bill. Video footage of his slow and agonizing death on the street in plain view showed him suffocating under the knee of Officer Derek Chauvin for over eight minutes, galvanizing many in the country and, indeed, around the world to protest against this horrific breach of the rule of law and due process.[24]

Finally, and first in this sequence of events, the white nationalist "Unite the Right" rally in Charlottesville, Virginia, on August 11, 2017, descended into mob violence that evening as a neo-Nazi motorist rammed his car into thirty-two-year-old Heather Heyer, killing her and injuring dozens of others. Two state police officers also lost their lives that night when their helicopter crashed while monitoring the scene.[25] The racist and antisemitic chants that accompanied the rally in the city best known for being Thomas Jefferson's home and the site of the university he founded were emblematic of the ascendancy of hatred and the loosening of attachments for democratic politics and rational discourse in recent years. "Passion has helped us," Lincoln said with respect to America's revolutionary founding, "but can do so no more. It will in future be our enemy." Charlottesville, Minneapolis, and Washington, DC, have become modern avatars for Vicksburg, St. Louis, and Alton.

The deaths related to these recent manifestations of mob violence were indeed minimized by President Donald Trump, who could neither condemn the perpetrators outright nor summon the will (or decency) to offer condolences to the victims. To make matters worse, only a small number of Republicans did so, and some of them would later recant their initial publicly expressed views. Of those few who have stood steadfast to the ideals of due process and the rule of law, Rep. Liz Cheney of Wyoming has been perhaps the most outspoken. Her September 22, 2022, speech at the American Enterprise Institute began with a reference to Lincoln's Lyceum Address.

> On January 6, as I walked into the room where members of Congress were being evacuated, my phone beeped. I was receiving a text message from a young woman named Jenna Lifhits. She was sending me Abraham Lincoln's Lyceum Address. Its message of reverence for the law could not have been timelier. It is a notion that I think of often.[26]

While Cheney did not quote directly from the Lyceum Address, her talk that day echoed many of Lincoln's sentiments. Indeed, the title of her lecture, "Our Constitutional Moment: The Danger to the Rule of Law," expressed Lincoln's concerns quite well. But her speech was also an object lesson for appreciating just how far Lincoln was willing to go in linking the events in Vicksburg to those in St. Louis and Alton. While Liz Cheney's condemnation of President Trump's behavior on January 6—and elsewhere—has been as sharp as any, she has not gone so far as to suggest that the spirit of mobocracy let loose on the nation's capital on January 6 belongs to the same genus that inspired the murder of George Floyd or the rampage in Charlottesville. Instead, she threw a barb at "radical liberalism and wokeness," leaving any discussion of race or white supremacy on the cutting room floor.[27]

Limiting the Lyceum Address's value to a rule-of-law speech shortchanges Lincoln, but more importantly, it shortchanges us. The interconnectedness of the downward spiral away from democracy with the rise of white supremacist violence is not only playing out in the United States, but also around the world—something that Lincoln would have seen as warranting great concern. Perhaps the unprecedented numbers of Americans of all colors and citizens from many cities around the world taking to the streets in the days after George Floyd's murder can offer some succor for a nation that seems to be able to only focus on one perceived threat to democracy at a time and, more often than not, quite poorly at that.

However employed, the resurgence of the Lyceum Address in recent years speaks to the darkness of our time. In one of the more eloquent recent invocations of the speech, Democratic Representative Jamie Raskin's of Maryland stands out. In his closing remarks of President Donald Trump's second impeachment trial, Raskin spoke from the heart about experiencing the horrors of the Capitol riot that sought to reverse the election results of 2020. His remarks are worth reviewing at length here:

> Distinguished members of the Senate, my youngest daughter, Tabitha, was there with me on Wednesday, January sixth. It was the day after we buried her brother, our son, Tommy, the saddest day of our lives. Also there was my son-in-law, Hank, who's married to our oldest daughter, Hannah. And I consider him a son, too, even though he eloped with my daughter and didn't tell us what they were going to do. But it was in the middle of COVID-19. But the reason they came with me that Wednesday, January sixth, was because they wanted to be together with me in the middle of a devastating week for our family. And I told them I had to go back to work because we were counting electoral votes that day, on January sixth. It was our constitutional duty. And I invited them instead to come with me to witness

this historic event: the peaceful transfer of power in America.

And they said they heard that President Trump was calling on his followers to come to Washington to protest. And they asked me directly, "Would it be safe? Would it be safe?" And I told them, "Of course it should be safe. This is the Capitol." Steny Hoyer, our majority leader, had kindly offered me the use of his office on the House floor, because I was one of the managers that day and we were going through our grief. So Tabitha and Hank were with me in Steny's office as colleagues dropped by to console us about the loss of our middle child, Tommy, our beloved Tommy. Mr. Neguse and Mr. Cicilline actually came to see me that day. Dozens of members—lots of Republicans, lots of Democrats—came to see me, and I felt a sense of being lifted up from the agony. And I won't forget their tenderness.

And through the tears, I was working on a speech for the floor, when we would all be together in joint session. And I wanted to focus on unity when we met in the House. I quoted Abraham Lincoln's famous 1838 Lyceum speech, where he said that if division and destruction ever come to America, it won't come from abroad; it will come from within. And in that same speech, Lincoln passionately deplored mob violence. This was right after the murder of Elijah Lovejoy, the abolitionist newspaper editor. And Lincoln deplored mob violence, and he deplored mob rule. And he said it would lead to tyranny and despotism in America.

Rep. Liz Cheney.

That was the speech I gave that day, after the House very graciously and warmly welcomed me back. And Tabitha and Hank came with me to the floor, and they watched it from the gallery. And when it was over, they went back to that office, Steny's office, off of the House floor. They didn't know that the House had been breached yet and that an insurrection or riot or a coup had come to Congress. And by the time we learned about it, about what was going on, it was too late. I couldn't get out there to be with them in that office. And all around me, people were calling their wives and their husbands, their loved ones to say goodbye. Members of Congress, in the House anyway, were removing their congressional pins so they wouldn't be identified by the mob as they tried to escape the violence. Our new chaplain got up and said a prayer for us. And we were told to put our gas masks on.

And then there was a sound I will never forget: the sound of pounding on the door like a battering ram. It's the most haunting sound I ever heard, and I will never forget it. My chief of staff, Julie Tagen, was with Tabitha and Hank, locked and barricaded in that office, the kids hiding under the desk, placing what they thought were their final texts and whispered phone calls to say their goodbyes. They thought they were going to die.

My son-in-law had never even been to the Capitol before. And when they were finally rescued, over an hour later, by Capitol officers and we were together, I hugged them, and I apologized. And I told my daughter, Tabitha, who's twenty-four and a brilliant algebra teacher in Teach for America now—I told her how sorry I was. And I promised her that it would not be like this again the next time she came back to the

Rep. Jamie Raskin.

> Capitol with me. And you know what she said? She said, "Dad, I don't want to come back to the Capitol."
>
> Of all the terrible, brutal things I saw and I heard on that day and since then, that one hit me the hardest, that and watching someone use an American flagpole, with the flag still on it, to spear and pummel one of our police officers ruthlessly, mercilessly—tortured by a pole with a flag on it that he was defending with his very life. People died that day. Officers ended up with head damage and brain damage. People's eyes were gouged. An officer had a heart attack. An officer lost three fingers that day. Two officers have taken their own lives.
>
> Senators, this cannot be our future. This cannot be the future of America. We cannot have presidents inciting and mobilizing mob violence against our government and our institutions because they refuse to accept the will of the people under the Constitution of the United States. Much less can we create a new January exception in our precious, beloved Constitution, that prior generations have died for and fought for, so that corrupt presidents have several weeks to get away with whatever it is they want to do. History does not support a January exception in any way. So why would we invent one for the future?[28]

Raskin's speech had a full-circle quality to it. An American president—a Caesar, if you like—had inspired a revolt against America's democratic institutions. The Capitol Building and its grounds resembled the chaos and violence more in keeping with a battlefield than the grand edifice of the world's greatest democracy. As is the case in times of crisis, we turn to words of comfort to get our moorings right, to somehow explain to ourselves what we are experiencing and to find a way forward. Raskin's speech that day was naturally covered extensively, given the circumstances, and more than one friend texted me as it unfolded, knowing I was writing a book on the Lyceum Address. "Are you watching this?" one wrote. I could muster no joy in the Lyceum's newfound popularity. I could only conjure an image from mythology in weighing Lincoln's prescience—and it haunts both then and now. It is the image of Cassandra, the Greek priestess whose gift for prophecy was true, but not believed. "I'm watching," I texted, slumping back into the couch.

FOUR MONTHS AFTER THE INAUGURATION OF JOE BIDEN AS president, the United States Congress approved nearly two billion dollars to fortify the Capitol.[29] Was this the nation's best response to Lincoln's question at the Lyceum—"By what means shall we fortify against it?—concerning the growing dangers to America's political institutions? The fortifications Lincoln deemed necessary were internal. Lincoln's call was to teach reverence for the laws and the virtues of self-government, over and over again; it had to become, as he put it, our "civil religion."

But Lincoln taught something else at the Lyceum that many are revolting against now, and that is the need to take a hard, cold look at the antidemocratic aspects of America's past. Sadly, among those who support Lincoln's reverence for the founders today are those who would likely oppose teaching the murders of Francis McIntosh and Elijah P. Lovejoy—and perhaps those hanged in Vicksburg. Lincoln's insistence in calling out the vile, hateful, and antidemocratic trends of his own time does not appear to be a lesson all are prepared to practice in our own time. The movement to remove "unpleasant" truths from American history in the nation's schools, especially those related to slavery and race, may be the worst movement away from Lincoln's message at the Lyceum, where he spoke eloquently and vividly about the killing of those on the periphery of American society. Today, whether it's in Alabama, where students recently walked out after being told they could not learn about slavery during Black History Month; or in South Carolina, where a state representative filed a bill to ban the "uncomfortable and upsetting" history of "slave owners"; or in Florida, where public school books have been banned because they create "guilt and anguish" in students (including *The Life of Rosa Parks*), the trend in at least part of the country has been to look away from the very ills Lincoln wanted us to see.[30] Indeed, it is no stretch to consider that the Lyceum Address, with its references to lynchings, burnings, and shootings related to race, might find itself removed from the shelves and discussions found in any number of America's public schools.

There is no denying Lincoln desperately wanted a love of America's Constitution to be cultivated. And he stressed the need in his Lyceum Address to educate future generations about the virtues of self-government and the rule of law. That he did so while deploring the "pleasure-hunting masters of Southern slaves," along with those who killed "Negroes and those thought to be leagued with Negroes," was an act of courage few, if any, of his contemporaries were willing to undertake. Now, 185 years later, similar courage remains appallingly sporadic. We are still trying to make peace with racism's incompatibility with democratic life, a fusion of values Lincoln thought to be essential from the very start of his political career.

"If Lincoln achieved greatness, he grew into it," the great historian Eric Foner has written.[31] But as novelist Ralph Ellison has reminded us, progress in history doesn't always move in a straight line; it rather moves, more often than we'd like to admit, like a boomerang, surprising us with its returns to form. The Lyceum Address foretold much of what was to come in a President Lincoln. His steadfastness against slavery's expansion; his belief in the interlocking relationship between self-government and racial justice; and his courage to do all to preserve the greatest principle enshrined in America's Constitution: equality for all before the law.

It is true that, in 1838, Lincoln lacked the experience and polish he would cultivate over the next few decades as a man and as a politician. But in taking the Lyceum Address into full account, by giving it its due—and the events that inspired it—we can see Lincoln the way instructors see their master pupils many years later. The years will undoubtedly have helped them to hone their talents, and the fullness of their greatness can only be best judged when in full possession of their powers. Nevertheless, upon careful review, the schoolmaster can see all of the important ingredients present in the beginning. It is, after all, what Lincoln believed about America—that its birth reflected all of the excellence in need of preservation and, indeed, expansion. And so it was, for the unheralded young politician standing before his neighbors and friends on a midwinter night, in a time of troubles.

APPENDIX A

"On the Perpetuation of Our Political Institutions"

ADDRESS BEFORE THE YOUNG MEN'S LYCEUM OF SPRINGFIELD, ILLINOIS

January 27, 1838

As a subject for the remarks of the evening, *the perpetuation of our political institutions,* is selected.

In the great journal of things happening under the sun, we, the American People, find our account running, under date of the nineteenth century of the Christian era.—We find ourselves in the peaceful possession, of the fairest portion of the earth, as regards extent of territory, fertility of soil, and salubrity of climate. We find ourselves under the government of a system of political institutions, conducing more essentially to the ends of civil and religious liberty, than any of which the history of former times tells us. We, when mounting the stage of existence, found ourselves the legal inheritors of these fundamental blessings. We toiled not in the acquirement or establishment of them—they are a legacy bequeathed us, by a *once* hardy, brave, and patriotic, but *now* lamented and departed race of ancestors. Theirs was the task (and nobly they performed it) to possess themselves, and through themselves, us, of this goodly land; and to uprear upon its hills and its valleys, a political edifice of liberty and equal rights; 'tis ours only, to transmit these, the former, unprofaned by the foot of an invader; the latter, undecayed by the lapse of time and untorn by usurpation, to the latest generation that fate shall permit the world to know. This task of gratitude to our fathers, justice to ourselves, duty to posterity, and love for our species in general, all imperatively require us faithfully to perform.

How then shall we perform it?—At what point shall we expect the approach of danger? By what means shall we fortify against it?—Shall we expect some transatlantic military giant, to step the Ocean, and crush us at a blow? Never!—All the armies of Europe, Asia, and Africa combined, with all the treasure of the earth (our own excepted) in their military chest; with a Buonaparte for a commander, could not by force, take a drink from the Ohio, or make a track on the Blue Ridge, in a trial of a thousand years.

At what point then is the approach of danger to be expected? I answer, if it ever reach us, it must spring up amongst us. It cannot come from abroad. If destruction be our lot, we must ourselves be its author and finisher. As a nation of freemen, we must live through all time, or die by suicide.

I hope I am over wary; but if I am not, there is, even now, something of ill-omen, amongst us. I mean the increasing disregard for law which pervades the country; the growing disposition to substitute the wild and furious passions, in lieu of the sober judgment of Courts; and the worse than savage mobs, for the executive ministers of justice. This disposition is awfully fearful in any community; and that it now exists in ours, though grating to our feelings to admit, it would be a violation of truth, and an insult to our intelligence, to deny. Accounts of outrages committed by mobs, form the every-day news of the times. They have pervaded the country, from New England to Louisiana;—they are neither peculiar to the eternal snows of the former, nor the burning suns of the latter;—they are not the creature of climate—neither are they confined to the slave-holding, or the non-slave-holding States. Alike, they spring up among the pleasure-hunting masters of Southern slaves, and the order-loving citizens of the land of steady habits.—Whatever, then, their cause may be, it is common to the whole country.

It would be tedious, as well as useless, to recount the horrors of all of them. Those happening in the State of Mississippi, and at St. Louis, are, perhaps, the most dangerous in example and revolting to humanity. In the Mississippi case, they first commenced by hanging the regular gamblers; a set of men, certainly not following for a livelihood, a very useful, or very honest occupation; but one which, so far from being forbidden by the laws, was actually licensed by an act of the Legislature, passed but a single year before. Next, negroes, suspected of conspiring to raise an insurrection, were caught up and hanged in all parts of the State; then, white men, supposed to be leagued with the negroes; and finally, strangers, from neighboring States, going thither on business, were, in many instances, subjected to the same fate. Thus went on this process of hanging, from gamblers to negroes, from negroes to white citizens, and from these to strangers; till, dead men were seen literally dangling from the boughs of trees upon every road side; and in numbers almost sufficient, to rival the native Spanish moss of the country, as a drapery of the forest.

Turn, then, to that horror-striking scene at St. Louis. A single victim was only sacrificed there. His story is very short; and is, perhaps, the most highly tragic, if anything of its length, that has ever been witnessed in real life. A mulatto man, by the name of McIntosh, was seized in the street, dragged to the suburbs of the city, chained to a tree, and actually burned to death; and all within a single hour from the time he had been a freeman, attending to his own business, and at peace with the world.

Such are the effects of mob law; and such as the scenes, becoming more and more frequent in this land so lately famed for love of law and order; and the stories of which, have even now grown too familiar, to attract any thing more, than an idle remark.

But you are, perhaps, ready to ask, "What has this to do with the perpetuation of our political institutions?" I answer, it has much to do with it. Its direct consequences are, comparatively speaking, but a small evil; and much of its danger consists, in the proneness of our minds, to regard its direct, as its only consequences. Abstractly considered, the hanging of the gamblers at Vicksburg, was of but little consequence. They constitute a portion of population, that is worse than useless in any community; and their death, if no pernicious example be set by it, is never matter of reasonable regret with any one. If they were annually swept, from the stage of existence, by the plague or small pox, honest men would, perhaps, be much profited, by the operation.—Similar too, is the correct reasoning, in regard to the burning of the negro at St. Louis. He had forfeited his life, by the perpetration of an outrageous murder, upon one of the most worthy and respectable citizens of the city; and had not he died as he did, he must have died by the sentence of the law, in a very short time afterwards. As to him alone, it was as well the way it was, as it could otherwise have been.—But the example in either case, was fearful.—When men take it in their heads to day, to hang gamblers, or burn murderers, they should recollect, that, in the confusion usually attending such transactions, they will be as likely to hang or burn some one who is neither a gambler nor a murderer as one who is; and that, acting upon the example they set, the mob of to-morrow, may, and probably will, hang or burn some of them by the very same mistake. And not only so; the innocent, those who have ever set their faces against violations of law in every shape, alike with the guilty, fall victims to the ravages of mob law; and thus it goes on, step by step, till all the walls erected for the defense of the persons and property of individuals, are trodden down, and disregarded. But all this even, is not the full extent of the evil.—By such examples, by instances of the perpetrators of such acts going unpunished, the lawless in spirit, are encouraged to become lawless in practice; and having been used to no restraint, but dread of punishment, they thus become, absolutely unrestrained.—Having ever regarded Government as their deadliest bane, they make a jubilee of the suspension of its operations; and pray for nothing so much, as its total annihilation. While, on the other hand, good men, men who love tranquility, who desire to abide by the laws, and enjoy their benefits, who would gladly spill their blood in the defense of their country; seeing their property destroyed; their families insulted, and their lives endangered; their persons injured; and seeing nothing in prospect that forebodes a change for the better; become tired of, and disgusted with, a Government that offers them no protection; and are not much averse to a change in which they imagine they have nothing to lose. Thus, then, by the operation of this mobocractic spirit, which all must admit, is now abroad in the land, the strongest bulwark of any Government, and particularly of those constituted like ours, may effectually be broken down and destroyed—I mean the *attachment* of the People. Whenever this effect shall be produced among us; whenever the vicious portion of population shall be permitted to gather in bands of hundreds and thousands, and burn churches, ravage and rob provision-stores, throw printing presses into rivers, shoot editors, and hang and burn obnoxious persons at pleasure, and with impunity; depend on it, this Government cannot last. By such things, the feelings of the best citizens will become more or less alienated from it; and thus it will be left without friends, or with too few, and those few too weak, to make their friendship effectual. At such a time and under such circumstances, men of sufficient talent and ambition will not be wanting to seize the opportunity, strike the blow, and overturn that fair fabric, which for the last half century, has been the fondest hope, of the lovers of freedom, throughout the world.

I know the American People are *much* attached to their Government;—I know they would suffer *much* for its sake;—I know they would endure evils long and patiently, before they would ever think of exchanging it for another. Yet, notwithstanding all this, if the laws be continually despised and disregarded, if their rights to be secure in their persons and property, are held by no better tenure than the caprice of a mob, the alienation of their affections from the Government is the natural consequence; and to that, sooner or later, it must come.

Here then, is one point at which danger may be expected.

The question recurs, "How shall we fortify against it?" The answer is simple. Let every American, every lover of liberty, every well-wisher to his posterity, swear by the blood of the Revolution, never to violate in the least particular, the laws of the country; and never to tolerate their violation by others. As the patriots of seventy-six did to the support of the Declaration of Independence, so to the support of the Constitution and Laws, let every American pledge his life, his property, and his sacred honor;—let every man remember that to violate the law, is to trample on the blood of his father, and to tear the character of his own, and his children's liberty. Let reverence for the laws, be breathed by every American mother, to the lisping babe, that prattles on her lap—let it be taught in schools, in seminaries, and in colleges; let it be written in Primers, spelling books, and in Almanacs;—let it be preached from the pulpit, proclaimed in legislative halls, and enforced in courts of justice. And, in short, let it become the *political religion* of the nation; and let the old and the young, the rich and the poor, the grave and the gay, of all sexes and tongues, and colors and conditions, sacrifice unceasingly upon its altars.

While ever a state of feeling, such as this, shall universally, or even, very generally prevail throughout the nation, vain will be every effort, and fruitless every attempt, to subvert our national freedom.

When I so pressingly urge a strict observance of all the laws, let me not be understood as saying there are no bad laws, nor that grievances may not arise, for the redress of which, no legal provisions have been made.—I mean to say no such thing. But I do mean to say, that, although bad laws, if they exist, should be repealed as soon as possible, still while they continue in force, for the sake of example, they should be religiously observed. So also in unprovided cases. If such arise, let proper legal provisions be made for them with the least possible delay; but, till then, let them, if not too intolerable, be borne with.

There is no grievance that is a fit object of redress by mob law. In any case that arises, as for instance, the promulgation of abolitionism, one of two positions is necessarily true; that is, the thing is right within itself, and therefore deserves the protection of all law and all good citizens; or, it is wrong, and therefore proper to be prohibited by legal enactments; and in neither case, is the interposition of mob law, either necessary, justifiable, or excusable.

But, it may be asked, why suppose danger to our political institutions? Have we not preserved them for more than fifty years? And why may we not for fifty times as long?

We hope there is *no sufficient* reason. We hope all dangers may be overcome; but to conclude that no danger may ever arise, would itself be extremely dangerous. There are now, and will hereafter be, many causes, dangerous in their tendency, which have not existed heretofore; and which are not too insignificant to merit attention. That our government should have been maintained in its original form from its establishment until now, is not much to be wondered at. It had many props to support it through that period, which now are decayed, and crumbled away. Through that period, it was felt by all, to be an undecided experiment; now, it is understood to be a successful one. Then, all that sought celebrity and fame, and distinction, expected to find them in the success of that experiment. Their *all* was staked upon it:—their destiny was *inseparably* linked with it. Their ambition aspired to display before an admiring world, a practical demonstration of the truth of a proposition, which had hitherto been considered, at best no better, than problematical; namely, *the capability of a people to govern themselves*. If they succeeded, they were to be immortalized; their names were to be transferred to counties and cities, and rivers and mountains; and to be revered and sung, and toasted through all time. If they failed, they were to be called knaves and fools, and fanatics for a fleeting hour; then to sink and be forgotten. They succeeded. The experiment is successful; and thousands have won their deathless names in making it so. But the game is caught; and I believe it is true, that with the catching, end the pleasures of the chase. This field of glory is harvested, and the crop is already appropriated. But new reapers will arise, and *they*, too, will seek a field. It is to deny, what the history of the world tells us is true, to suppose that men of ambition and talents will not continue to spring up amongst us. And, when they do, they will as naturally seek the gratification of their ruling passion, as others have so done before them. The question then, is, can that gratification be found in supporting and maintaining an edifice that has been erected by others? Most certainly it cannot. Many great and good men sufficiently qualified for any task they should undertake, may ever be found, whose ambition would inspire to nothing beyond a seat in Congress, a gubernatorial or a presidential chair; *but such belong not to the family of the lion, or the tribe of the eagle.* What! think you these places would satisfy an Alexander, a Caesar, or a Napoleon?—Never! Towering genius distains a beaten path. It seeks regions hitherto unexplored.—It sees *no distinction* in adding story to story, upon the monuments of fame, erected to the memory of others. It *denies* that it is glory enough to serve under any chief. It *scorns* to tread in the footsteps of *any* predecessor, however illustrious. It thirsts and burns for distinction; and, if possible, it will have it, whether at the expense of emancipating slaves, or enslaving freemen. Is it unreasonable then to expect, that some man possessed of the loftiest genius, coupled with ambition sufficient to push it to its utmost stretch, will at some time, spring up among us? And when such a one does, it will require the people to be united with each other, attached to the government and laws, and generally intelligent, to successfully frustrate his designs.

Distinction will be his paramount object, and although he would as willingly, perhaps more so, acquire it by doing good as harm; yet, that opportunity being past, and nothing left to be done in the way of building up, he would set boldly to the task of pulling down.

Here, then, is a probable case, highly dangerous, and such a one as could not have well existed heretofore.

Another reason which *once was*; but which, to the same extent, is *now no more*, has done much in maintaining our institutions thus far. I mean the powerful influence which the interesting scenes of the revolution had upon the *passions* of the people as distinguished from their judgment. By this influence, the jealousy, envy, and avarice, incident to our nature, and so common to a state of peace, prosperity, and conscious strength, were, for the time, in a great measure smothered and rendered inactive; while the deep-rooted principles of *hate*, and the powerful motive of *revenge*, instead of being turned against each other, were directed exclusively against the British nation. And thus, from the force of circumstances, the basest principles of our nature, were either made to lie dormant, or to become the active agents in the advancement of the noblest cause—that of establishing and maintaining civil and religious liberty.

But this state of feeling *must fade, is fading, has faded*, with the circumstances that produced it.

I do not mean to say, that the scenes of the revolution *are now* or *ever will* be entirely forgotten; but that like every thing else, they must fade upon the memory of the world, and grow more and more dim by the lapse of time. In history, we hope, they will be read of, and recounted, so long as the bible shall be read;—but even granting that they will, their influence *cannot be* what it heretofore has been. Even then, they *cannot be* so universally known, nor so vividly felt, as they were by the generation just gone to rest. At the close of that struggle, nearly every adult male had been a participator in some of its scenes. The consequence was, that of those scenes, in the form of a husband, a father, a son or brother, a *living history* was to be found in every family—a history bearing the indubitable testimonies of its own authenticity, in the limbs mangled, in the scars of wounds received, in the midst of the very scenes related—a history, too, that could be read and understood alike by all, the wise and the ignorant, the learned and the unlearned. But *those* histories are gone. They *can* be read no more forever. They *were* a fortress of strength; but, what invading foeman could *never do*, the silent artillery of time *has done*; the leveling of its walls. They are gone. They *were* a forest of giant oaks; but the all-resistless hurricane has swept over them, and left only, here and there, a lonely trunk, despoiled of its verdure, shorn of its foliage; unshading and unshaded, to murmur in a few gentle breezes, and to combat with its mutilated limbs, a few more ruder storms, then to sink, and be no more.

They *were* the pillars of the temple of liberty; and now, that they have crumbled away, that temple must fall, unless we, their descendants, supply their places with other pillars, hewn from the solid quarry of sober reason. Passion has helped us; but can do so no more. It will in future be our enemy. Reason, cold, calculating, unimpassioned reason, must furnish all the materials for our future support and defence.—Let those materials be moulded into *general intelligence, sound morality*, and in particular, *a reverence for the constitution and laws*: and, that we improved to the last; that we remained free to the last; that we revered his name to the last; that, during his long sleep, we permitted no hostile foot to pass over or desecrate his resting place; shall be that which to learn the last trump shall awaken our Washington.

Upon these let the proud fabric of freedom rest, as the rock of its basis; and as truly as has been said of the only greater institution, "*the gates of hell shall not prevail against it.*"

APPENDIX B

WILLIAM M. STEWART'S ADDRESS, DELIVERED AT THE UNION GROVE MEETING HOUSE IN PUTNAM COUNTY, ILLINOIS.

PUBLISHED IN THE *SANGAMO JOURNAL*, AUGUST 6, 1836. [THE AUTHOR HAS TAKEN THE LIBERTY TO MAKE MINOR CHANGES IN SPELLING AND GRAMMAR.]

William M. Stewart's July 4, 1836, message would be published in the Sangamo Journal *a year and a half before Abraham Lincoln would cover the same terrain in his Lyceum Address. Stewart, a white, New England–born abolitionist and cofounder of the Putnam County Anti-Slavery Society, brought his fiery opposition to slavery with him into Illinois. His speech, delivered on the sixtieth anniversary of the Declaration of Independence, was a powerful Christian attack on slavery and the hypocrisies it necessitated in American democracy. Taking the murders in Vicksburg and the burning of Francis McIntosh as his point of departure from America's founding roots in self-government, Stewart offers a scathing critique on racism, slavery, and mob violence. If not the basis for Lincoln's remarks at the Lyceum, Stewart's speech is a guide to how Lincoln would take the same moral stance and secularize it—calling for a "civil religion" at the Lyceum—to achieve the same goals Stewart laid out so passionately here.*

July 4, 1836

Sixty years ago to-day, these United States formally declared themselves free and independent; and from that time to the present, the citizens of this nation have enjoyed more liberty and greater privileges than the people of any other nation; and the debt of gratitude we owe to the most High is proportionally great.

My first object will be to show that Christians ought to be patriots; and that the sentiment which prevails to some extent among Christians, that they are at liberty to neglect public affairs as unworthy of their notice, is false and ought to be frowned on by everyone who participates in the blessings of this government.

Paul was a patriot, and his feelings on this subject were such as every citizen in our country ought to possess.—He says, "Brethren, my heart's desire and prayer to God for my country is that it may be saved." Yes. Saved from divisions and distractions in her councils; from disgust, tumults, and broils at home and contempt abroad; from civil and foreign wars; and finally saved with an everlasting salvation. Such no doubt was the breathings of St. Paul's patriotism, and such, to some extent, every generous mind will manifest. Nor is this love of country to be a secondary consideration, for this same apostle says again, "I exhort, therefore, that first of all, supplications, prayers, intercessions, and giving of thanks be made for all men. For Kings and all that are in authority; that we may lead a quiet and peaceable life, in all godliness and honesty. For this is good and acceptable in the sight of God our Saviour." Nor yet are we permitted to neglect or refuse to pray for those who are in authority, because we do not like the men or approve their official doings.—True it is our privilege (and a great privilege it is) to remove men from office by impeachment, or at the polls to change them for others; but so long as men are in authority we are to pray for them, sustain them, and use our influence to have them do their duty as public officers. And this we are to do, "that we may lead peaceable and quiet lives in all godliness and honesty."

How important it is that Christians be peaceable and honest and not disgrace their country or their religion by encouraging a contrary course of conduct by precept or example. Mobs, tumults, and insurrections are alike contrary the good of the community, the spirit of our free institutions, and the religion of the Bible. It is much better that a wicked man should go unpunished than that he should be punished in an unlawful way; for the law is the expressed will of the people, and to depart from it by doing more or less is wrong, except in matters of conscience; for all will allow that we may obey God rather than man. But a man must be very positive that God does not require it before he is at liberty to depart from the law of his country. For the command is very plain, Rom. 13, "let every soul be subject to the higher powers. For there is no power but from God. Whoever therefore resisteth the power, resisteth the ordinance of God; and they that resist shall receive to themselves damnation. For rulers are not a terror to good works but to the evil. Wilt thou then not be afraid of the power; do that which is good, and thou shall have praise of the same. For he is the minister of God to thee for good; but if thou dost that which is evil be afraid, for he heareth not the sword in vain; for he is a minister of God, an avenger to execute wrath on him that doeth evil. Wherefore ye must needs be subject not only for wrath but for conscience sake. For, for this cause ye pay tribute also; for they are God's ministers attending continually on this very thing; render therefore to all their dues; tribute to whom tribute is due; custom to whom custom; fear to whom fear; honor to whom honor." If then it is duty to submit to the laws of the land, it is also duty to take a deep interest in having those laws what they ought to be.

Every citizen of this nation is bound by the social compact, to be good and orderly, to love his country, obey or submit to her laws, and to promote her peace, prosperity, and honor. But to those duties the Christian is additionally bound by bis religion.

In this Government, Christians as such enjoy greater privileges than they do in any other, which is of itself a strong reason why they should be patriots.

The fourth day of July has, from the year '76, been celebrated by this nation as the birthday of its independence; and so far, this is as it should be. But July celebrations are objected to by many good men on account of the light and frothy addresses, and fooleries of these occasions. Brethren, if God and the cause of liberty are not honored by commemorating our independence, I ask whose fault it is? Surely it must be laid to the charge of those who know so well how it ought to be done, and yet will not devote to it the necessary time to make such occasions interesting and profitable. You cannot plead that it is an idle or foolish way of spending time, for this would be contrary to all Bible analogy on this subject; nor can you plead the circumstances which attended the declaration of independence, the revolutionary efforts, the subsequent success and freedom of the nation; or cur present condition, and future prospects; as an excuse for refusing to honor the annual return of freedom's birth day. For alter all the objections that can be made against this government it is by far the wisest and best in the world. Nothing can exceed it for simplicity, justice, and the equal proportion of all its parts. It far out . . . [illegible: page is torn] . . . near its match. But I will not be understood as saying a word derogatory to the talent and wisdom of our revolutionary statesmen; by no means. For it is my cool and deliberate opinion that as politicians they have not been equaled before or since.

Yet I am willing to give God the glory, and I believe it the duty of this from time to time to make a public acknowledgement of his goodness in our liberty, and also to honor those brave who secured the blessing instrumentally. But a word to all.

A few years since our fathers were a few families widely scattered through a wide wilderness, but off from the old world and in the new, surrounded by extensive forests, the beasts of prey, and the savage tribes. But rich themselves, having the Bible, the sabbath, and the fear of God. Now we are a great nation, with civil and religious privileges, and with resources for wealth, intelligence, and independence surpassing any other people. But we might, and ought, and must be, a much greater nation than we are: and this may be affected with perfect ease and safety in the following way, viz: let every man be as just and as good as his nature is capable of being, then we would be possessed of that true greatness to which all ought to aspire. Let everyone in this nation be industrious, frugal, moral, and intelligent, then certain happiness, prosperity, and honor would be our sure reward: and, in fact, every man is bound in honor, to contribute his full share toward securing for his country this glory and renown. But the man who chooses to be ignorant and vicious, chooses to be a bad citizen, he chooses to be that which, if all were like him, would destroy any country.

To parents and those who have the care of children and youths, I would say, as you love your country, teach them the "fear of God, which is the beginning of wisdom," and also the first principle of government, that "all men are born free and equal." Teach them to regard the rights of others and to observe the strictest rules of justice and honor in all their dealings with mankind.

To young men, I would say, aim at your country's honor, let her highest expectation in you be fully realized, and never suffer your conduct in the least to tarnish her character or lower her dignity.

Let everyone act in all things as if the destinies of his country depended on him; the nation is made up of individuals, and just what their character is, so will be that of the nation. It is the duty of everyone to encourage the universal diffusion of useful knowledge, and to be actuated in all his conduct by a principle of love to mankind for all the advantages we enjoy. If the people corrupt and not influenced by patriotic principles, our country must come to ruin and disgrace. But if our people pursue a virtuous and dignified course of conduct, in their public and private acts, then will peace, long life, and prosperity be the certain portion of this Republic.

But the story of our beloved country has a dark side to it, and justice requires that it should also be seen. A stranger to hear of our revolutionary wars and sufferings but a little more than half a century ago, and the sacrifices made for the cause of liberty by the heroes, heroines, statesmen, and generals of that memorable period, then to see our excellent constitution, our schools, colleges, universities throughout the length and breadth of the land; and hear the ten thousand times ten thousand, warm and patriotic demands, teaming forth in every quarter of our country, from the July oration, the pulpit, the press, and every grade of office hunters, to reverence the wisdom and justice of our government and the freedom and consequent happiness of the people: I say, if a stranger to become acquainted with our history, he would be very apt to conclude that their land is nearly allied to paradise; in which there are no tyrants or oppression but good will to man and an ardent desire for universal liberty burns with unquenchable fire in the breast of every citizen. But is such the fact? Is every citizen of this republic a dear lover of liberty and equal rights? By no means. Many of our highly honored and gifted men, who are flaming republicans, are at this time engaged in the vile practice of buying and selling their fellows for gain; lording it over their liberties and consciences with inexpressible cruelty, and yet would esteem it a gross insult to be charged with any want, of genuine republicanism.—Shame on such men and the people who would sustain them. Such instances of depravity go to show that "the heart is deceitful above all things and desperately wicked; who can know it?" Where are our boasted rights? The strong arm of the law in many places has become weak and is no longer adequate to the task of protection: The wicked and worthless man and the excellent of the earth are equally liable to the outrages of the ruthless mob. Look at Vicksburgh [sp] and St. Louis, where men were put to death in a cruel and wanton manner, in direct violation of the laws of the country. True they were charged with gambling and murder, but men must be under a very strong paroxysm of morality who would murder their neighbors to suppress gambling. And on the other side, look at those truly Great and excellent men, ("of whom the world is not worthy") such as Nelson, Birnie, and Lovejoy: persecuted and driven from place to place, against whom not a shadow of a charge could be brought, except that they were republicans, or in other words, they were lovers of liberty, and like our forefathers were bold and honest enough to speak against tyranny and defend the cause of the poor and oppressed American.

One sixth part of this nation is enslaved and degraded to a most shocking degree. [illegible: page is torn] . . . the United States could make sixty States as populous as Illinois was when it was received into the Union; and this great nation of people, though innocent and harmless to an uncommon degree, is much more oppressed and degraded than our fathers were before the revolution, or than the Irish, the Greeks, or the Poles were in their late struggles for their just rights. Yet if a man in this land of freedom should say a word for the oppressed slave; should open his mouth for the dumb and plead for two millions of his fellows; who are compelled to wear a yoke more galling than ever chafed the necks of any people, he has committed a crime for which, in the opinion of many, he may be lynched, or put to an ignoble death. Thousands of dollars have been publicly offered in the face of law and justice, for the heads of uncondemned American freemen against whom no crime was alleged, except an uncompromising love for our free institutions, and for manifesting a desire that every American should participate in their glorious privileges.—Many presses have been demolished for no other fault than defending our National charter, and the rights of her insulted people.—Mob after mob has been raised for the express purpose of suppressing the free discussion of great questions; questions where the rights of the poor and the oppressed were involved. And many prudent and well-meaning men have been publicly libeled and slandered and charged through the length and breath of the land, when guilty of no offence in the eyes of the law whatever, nor of any other offence except loving and defending the very principles on which our government is based, and for which our fathers spilt their dearest blood; and which is now dear to every lover of liberty. A man must be blind indeed who does not see that American slavery is naturally, morally, and politically wrong; that in it the spirit and principles of our government are blackguarded; and that a nation, as an individual, cannot be placed in a more ridiculous attitude than while, claiming to be republicans, they profess the principle and are in the practice of slavery; yet such is the fact in our case.—I ask again where is our boasted American liberty that stands so dignified in person, so honored in letters, and so profoundly reverenced by historians, poets, and speechmakers throughout the world.

Many states in this Union have enacted laws and based every other possible means of instruction which they enjoy to the full; and from the possession of every other right and privilege which is necessary to constitute a freeman: and in addition to this, they heap on them evert insult, injury, and cruelty which the ingenuity of unrestrained demons incarnate can invent. What extreme infatuation. "Will not God be avenged on such a nation as this?" May we not with Jefferson tremble for our country when we reflect, that God has no one attribute that will take sides with us on the subject of slavery. In slavery, every law of God is transgressed, and every principle of kindness and common honesty is trampled underfoot. And I am bold to affirm that the man who does most to sustain slavery is the greatest tyrant and ought to be esteemed the worst enemy to his country. For it would be just as reasonable to hope that a magazine of powder could be preserved while fire is continually flashing in its midst as that this nation can be preserved in peace with the present system of slavery in its bosom.

On this occasion I have taken the liberty to speak freely on the subject of slavery because it is the all-absorbing question, and because we are in common with all our sister states deeply interested in the result. I will now conclude with a few remarks.

1. There is hope in our cause because the spirit and principles of our government are wise and sound, and if suffered to work, they will root out slavery most thoroughly.
2. There is no sense in which slavery is the fault of our plan of Government; for it was prior to it, and has ever been, in direct violation of the plan and design of our free institutions.
3. There are no doubt many wrong views on the subject of slavery and the best way to get clear of it, but perhaps there is none more dangerous than the common action, which is to "let it alone."
4. I suppose it capable of proof that no moral power in the united world except that of the church could sustain slavery; and that those efforts that produce a change in the character of the church on this subject are the only efforts that do anything to remove slavery.
5. As it is an object worthy of the zeal and labor of every citizen of our country, to promote her happiness; let wisdom and sound policy, have a word to say in the choice of means.— Give learning and the Bible to all the people. Our government cannot be sustained without virtue and intelligence; these cannot be sustained without Christian religion, nor this without the Bible, the sabbath, and the ordinances of God's house. That God may bless you and this nation, with peace and great prosperity at home; and with deserved honor for wisdom and justice abroad, is the prayer of your fellow citizen.

APPENDIX C

The "House Divided" Speech, Springfield, Illinois

While Lincoln would hone his oratorical skills over the twenty years after delivering the Lyceum Address, he would return to the same themes established in that first, major speech. By 1858, the mob violence and dissolution of democratic values—if not America's democracy itself—were at hand. The Kansas–Nebraska Act (1854), along with the Dred Scott decision (1857), made civil war all the more likely. Here, in June of 1858, Lincoln, now running for senator, delivers an address at the Republican party nominating convention in Springfield. Lincoln would go on to lose the race to Illinois's Stephen A. Douglas, whose debates with Lincoln in the coming months would later be memorialized. Yet the House Divided Speech would come to define Lincoln as not only a gifted speaker but, indeed, one with a prophetic message. Borrowing from its first appearance in the Book of Matthew, Lincoln uses the metaphor of a divided house to explain the nature of the present crisis before the American people, and why slavery is at the heart of it.

June 16, 1858

Mr. President and Gentlemen of the Convention.

If we could first know *where* we are, and *whither* we are tending, we could better judge *what* to do, and *how* to do it.

We are now far into the fifth year since a policy was initiated with the *avowed* object, and *confident* promise, of putting an end to slavery agitation.

Under the operation of that policy, that agitation has not only *not ceased* but has *constantly augmented.*

In *my* opinion, it *will* not cease until a *crisis* shall have been reached, and passed—

"A house divided against itself cannot stand."

I believe this government cannot endure, permanently half *slave* and half *free.*

I do not expect the Union to be *dissolved*—I do not expect the house to *fall*—but I do expect it will cease to be divided.

It will become *all* one thing, or *all* the other.

Either the *opponents* of slavery will arrest the further spread of it and place it where the public mind shall rest in the belief that it is in course of ultimate extinction; or its *advocates* will push it forward till it shall become alike lawful in *all* the States, old as well as new, *North* as well as *South.*

Have we no *tendency* to the latter condition?

Let anyone who doubts carefully contemplate that now almost complete legal combination—piece of *machinery,* so to speak—compounded of the Nebraska doctrine and the Dred Scott decision. Let him consider not only *what work* the machinery is adapted to do, and how well adapted, but also let him study the *history* of its construction and trace, if he can—or rather *fail,* if he can—the evidences of design and concert of action among its chief bosses, from the beginning.

But, so far, *Congress* only had acted; and an *indorsement* by the people, *real* or apparent, was indispensable, to *save* the point already gained, and give chance for more.

The new year of 1854 found slavery excluded from more than half the State-by-State Constitutions, and from most of the national territory by congressional prohibition.

Four days later, commenced the struggle, which ended in repealing that congressional prohibition.

This opened all the national territory to slavery and was the first point gained.

This necessity had not been overlooked, but had been provided for, as well as might be, in the notable argument of "*squatter sovereignty*," otherwise called "*sacred right of self-government*," which the latter phrase, though expressive of the only rightful basis of any government, was so perverted in this attempted use of it as to amount to just this: That if any *one* man choose to enslave *another*, no *third* man shall be allowed to object.

That argument was incorporated into the Nebraska bill itself, in the language which follows: "*It being the true intent and meaning of this act not to legislate slavery into any Territory or State, nor to exclude it therefrom; but to leave the people thereof perfectly free to form and regulate their domestic institutions in their own way, subject only to the Constitution of the United States.*"

Then opened the roar of loose declamation in favor of "squatter sovereignty" and "sacred right of self-government."

"But," said opposition members, "let us be more *specific*. Let us amend the bill so as to expressly declare that the people of the Territory *may* exclude slavery."

"Not we," said the friends of the measure, and down they voted the amendment.

While the Nebraska bill was passing through Congress, a *law case*, involving the question of a negro's freedom, by reason of his owner having voluntarily taken him first into a free State, and then a territory covered by the congressional prohibition and held him as a slave for a long time in each, was passing through the US Circuit Court for the District of Missouri; and both the Nebraska bill and lawsuit were brought to a decision in the same month of May 1854. The negro's name was Dred Scott, whose name now designates the decision finally made in the case.

Before the *then* next presidential election, the law case came to and was argued in the Supreme Court of the United States; but the *decision* of it was deferred until *after* the election. Still, *before* the election, Senator Trumbull, on the floor of the Senate, requests the leading advocate of the Nebraska bill to state his *opinion* whether the people of a territory can constitutionally exclude slavery from their limits; and the latter answers, "That is a question for the Supreme Court."

The election came. Mr. Buchanan was elected, and the indorsement, such as it was, secured. That was the *second point* gained. The indorsement, however, fell short of a clear popular majority by nearly four hundred thousand votes, and so, perhaps, was not overwhelmingly reliable and satisfactory.

The *outgoing* President, in his last annual message, as impressively as possible, *echoed back* upon the people the *weight* and *authority* of the indorsement.

The Supreme Court met again, *did not* announce their decision, but ordered a re-argument.

The presidential inauguration came, and still no decision of the court; but the *incoming* President, in his inaugural address, fervently exhorted the people to abide by the forthcoming decision, *whatever it might be*.

Then, in a few days, came the decision.

The reputed author of the Nebraska bill finds an early occasion to make a speech at this Capitol indorsing the Dred Scott decision and vehemently denouncing all opposition to it.

The new President, too, seizes the early occasion of the Silliman letter to *indorse* and strongly *construe* that decision, and to express his astonishment than any different view had ever been entertained.

At length, a squabble springs up between the President and the author of the Nebraska bill on the *mere* question of *fact*, whether the Lecompton Constitution was or was not, in any just sense, made by the people of Kansas; and in that quarrel, the latter declares that all he wants is a fair vote for the people and that he *cares* not whether slavery be voted down or voted up. I do not understand his declaration that he cares not whether slavery be voted *down* or voted *up*, to be intended by him other than as an *apt definition* of the policy he would impress upon the public mind—the *principle* for which he declares he has suffered much and is ready to suffer to the end. And well may he cling to that principle. If he has any parental feeling, well may he cling to it.

That principle is the only *shred* left of his original Nebraska doctrine. Under the Dred Scott decision, "squatter sovereignty" squatted out of existence, tumbled down like temporary scaffolding—like the mold at the foundry served through one blast and fell back into loose sand—helped to carry an election and then was kicked to the winds. His late *joint* struggle with the Republicans, against the Lecompton Constitution, involves nothing of the original Nebraska doctrine. That struggle was made on a point, the right of a people to make their own constitution, upon which he and the Republicans have never differed.

The several points of the Dred Scott decision, in connection with Senator Douglas's "care not" policy, constitute the piece of machinery in its present state of advancement.

The *working* points of that machinery are:

First, that no negro slave, imported as such from Africa, and no descendant of such slave can ever be a *citizen* of any State, in the sense of that term as used in the Constitution of the United States.

This point is made in order to deprive the negro, in every possible event, of the benefit of that provision of the United States Constitution, which declares that "the citizens of each State shall be entitled to all privileges and immunities of citizens in the several States."

Secondly, that "subject to the Constitution of the United States," neither *Congress* nor a *Territorial Legislature* can exclude slavery from any United States Territory.

This point is made in order that individual men may *fill up* the territories with slaves, without danger of losing them as property, and thus enhance the chances of *permanency* to the institution through all the future.

Thirdly, that whether the holding a negro in actual slavery in a free State makes him free, as against the holder, the United States courts will not decide but will leave to be decided by the courts of any slave State the negro may be forced into by the master.

This point is made, not to be pressed *immediately* but, if acquiesced in for a while, and apparently indorsed by the people at an election, then to sustain the logical conclusion that what Dred Scott's master might lawfully do with Dred Scott, in the free State of Illinois, every other master may lawfully do with any other *one* or one *thousand* slaves in Illinois, or in any other free State.

Auxiliary to all this, and working hand in hand with it, the Nebraska doctrine, or what is left of it, is to *educate* and *mould* public opinion, at least *Northern* public opinion, to not *care* whether slavery is voted *down* or voted *up*.

This shows exactly where we now *are*; and *partially* also, whither we are tending.

It will throw additional light on the latter, to go back and run the mind over the string of historical facts already stated. Several things will *now* appear less *dark* and *mysterious* than they did *when* they were transpiring. The people were to be left "perfectly free," "subject only to the Constitution." What the *Constitution* had to do with it, outsides could not *then* see. Plainly enough *now*, it was an exactly fitted *nitch* for the Dred Scott decision to afterward come in, and declare that *perfect freedom* of the people, to be just no freedom at all.

Why was the amendment, expressly declaring the right of the people to exclude slavery, voted down? Plainly enough *now*, the adoption of it, would have spoiled the nitch for the Dred Scott decision.

Why was the court decision held up? Why, even a senator's individual opinion withheld, till *after* the presidential election? Plainly enough *now*, the speaking out *then* would have damaged the "*perfectly free*" argument upon which the election was to be carried.

Why the *outgoing* President's felicitation on the indorsement? Why the delay of a re-argument? Why the incoming President's *advance* exhortation in favor of the decision?

These things *look* like the cautious *patting* and *petting* of a spirited horse, preparatory to mounting him, when it is dreaded that he may give the rider a fall.

Any why the hasty after indorsements of the decision by the President and others?

We cannot absolutely *know* that all these exact adaptations are the result of preconcert. But when we see a lot of framed timbers, different potions of which we know have been gotten out at different times and places and by different workmen—Stephen, Franklin, Roger and James, for instance—and we see these timbers joined together and see they exactly make the frame of a house or a mill, all the tenons and mortieses exactly fitting, and all the lengths and proportions of the different pieces exactly adapted to their respective places, and not a piece too many or too few—not omitting even scaffolding—or, if a single piece be lacking, we see the place in the frame exactly fitted and prepared to yet bring such piece in—in *such* a case, we find it impossible not to believe that Stephen and Franklin and Roger and James all understood one another from the beginning, and all worked upon a common *plan* or *draft* drawn up before the first lick was struck.

It should not be overlooked that, by the Nebraska bill, the people of *State*, as well as *Territory*, were to be left "*perfectly free*" and "*subject only to the Constitution.*"

Why mention a *State*? They were legislating for *territories*, and not *for* or *about* States. Certainly the people of a State *are* and *ought to be subject* to the Constitution of the United States; but why is mention of this *lugged* into this merely *territorial* law? Why are the people of a *territory* and the people of a *state* therein *lumped* together, and their relation to the Constitution therein treated as being *precisely* the same?

While the opinion of *the Court*, by Chief Justice Taney, in the Dred Scott case, and the separate opinions of all the concurring Judges, expressly declare that the Constitution of the United States neither permits Congress nor a territorial legislature to exclude slavery from any United States territory, they all *omit* to declare whether or not the same Constitution permits a *State*, or the people of a State, to exclude it.

Possibly, this is a mere *omission*; but who can be quite sure, if McLean or Curtis had sought to get into the opinion a declaration of unlimited power in the people of a *State* to exclude slavery from their limits, just as Chase and Mace sought to get such declaration, in behalf of the people of a territory, into the Nebraska bill—I ask, who can be quite *sure* that it would not have been voted down, in the one case, as it had been in the other?

The nearest approach to the point of declaring the power of a State over slavery is made by Judge Nelson. He approaches it more than once, using the precise idea, and *almost* the language, too, of the Nebraska act. On one occasion, his exact language is, "except in cases where the power is restrained by the Constitution of the United States, the law of the State is supreme over the subject of slavery within its jurisdiction."

In what *cases* the power of the *states* is so restrained by the US Constitution is left an *open* question, precisely as the same question, as to the restraint on the power of the *territories* was left open in the Nebraska act. Put *that* and *that* together, and we have another nice little nitch, which we may, ere long, see filled with another Supreme Court decision, declaring that the Constitution of the United States does not permit a *state* to exclude slavery from its limits.

And this may be expected if the doctrine of "care not whether slavery be voted *down* or voted *up*" shall gain upon the public mind sufficiently to give promise that such a decision can be maintained when made.

Such a decision is all that slavery now lacks of being alike lawful in all the States.

Welcome or unwelcome, such decision is probably coming, and will soon be upon us, unless the power of the present political dynasty shall be met and overthrown.

We shall *lie down* pleasantly dreaming that the people of *Missouri* are on the verge of making their State *free*; and we shall *awake* to the *reality*, instead, that the *Supreme* Court has made *Illinois a slave State*.

To meet and overthrow the power of that dynasty is the work now before all those who would prevent that consummation.

That is *what* we have to do.

But *how* can we best do it?

There are those who denounce us *openly* to their *own* friends, and yet whisper us *softly*, that Senator Douglas is the aptest instrument there is, with which to effect that object. *They* do *not* tell us, nor has *he* told us, that he *wishes* any such object to be affected. They wish us to *infer* all, from the facts, that he now has a little quarrel with the present head of the dynasty; and that he has regularly voted with us, on a single point, upon which, he and we, have never differed.

They remind us that *he* is a *great man*, and that the largest of *us* are very small ones. Let this be granted. But "a *living dog* is better than a *dead lion*." Judge Douglas, if not a *dead* lion *for this work*, is at least a *caged* and *toothless* one. How can he oppose the advance of slavery? He don't *care* anything about it. His avowed *mission is impressing* the "public heart" to *care* nothing about it.

A leading Douglas Democratic newspaper thinks Douglas's superior talent will be needed to resist the revival of the African slave trade.

Does Douglas believe an effort to revive that trade is approaching? He has not said so. Does he *really* think so? But if it is, how can he resist it? For years he has labored to prove it a *sacred right* of white men to take negro slaves into the new territories. Can he possibly show that it is *less* a sacred right to *buy* them where they can be brought cheapest? And, unquestionably, they can be bought *cheaper in Africa* than in *Virginia.*

He has done all in his power to reduce the whole question of slavery to one of a mere *right of property*; and, as such, how can *he* oppose the foreign slave trade—how can he refuse that trade in that "property" shall be "perfectly free"—unless he does it as a *protection* to the home production? And as the home *producers* will probably not *ask* the protection, he will be wholly without a ground of opposition.

Senator Douglas holds, we know, that a man may rightfully be *wiser today* than he was *yesterday*—that he may rightfully *change* when he finds himself wrong.

But, can we, for that reason, run ahead and *infer* that he will make any particular change, of which he, himself, has given no intimation? Can we *safely* base *our* action upon any such *vague* inference?

Now, as ever, I wish to not *misrepresent* Judge Doulgas's *position*, question his *motives*, or do aught that can be personally offensive to him.

Whenever, *if ever*, he and we can come together on *principle* so that *our great cause* may have assistance from *his great ability*, I hope to have interposed no adventitious obstacle.

But clearly, he is not *now* with us—he does not *pretend* to be—he does not *promise* to ever be.

Our cause, then, must be entrusted to, and conducted by, its own undoubted friends—those whose hands are free, whose hearts are in the work, who *do care* for the result.

Two years ago, the Republicans of the nation mustered over thirteen hundred thousand strong.

We did this under the single impulse of resistance to a common danger, with every external circumstance against us.

Of *strange*, *discordant*, and even *hostile* elements, we gathered from the four winds and *formed* and fought the battle through, under the constant hot fire of a disciplined, proud, and pampered enemy.

Did we brave all *then* to *falter* now? Now, when that same enemy is *wavering*, dissevered, and belligerent?

This result is not doubtful. We shall not fail—if we stand firm, we shall not fail.

Wise counsels may *accelerate* or *mistakes delay* it, but sooner or later, the victory is *sure* to come.

APPENDIX D

The Gettysburg Address, Gettysburg, Pennsylvania

Along with the Declaration of Independence, Lincoln's Gettysburg Address is the most eloquent, lauded, and refined statement of the deepest aspirations for American democracy. Delivered twenty-five years after the Lyceum Address, Lincoln returns to and crystallizes the themes he focused on in his first truly national address: the role of America's founding fathers, the violent crisis at hand threatening a return to a state of political harmony, and the need for a transformative politics that values every American's rights and humanity. At 272 words, it is more of a prayer ("Our fathers . . .") or oath than speech. Its brevity, wisdom, and meaning has become the subject of import for every succeeding generation since its delivery.

November 19, 1863

Four score and seven years ago, our fathers brought forth, on this continent, a new nation, conceived in Liberty and dedicated to the proposition that all men are created equal.

Now we are engaged in a great civil war, testing whether that nation, or any nation so conceived and so dedicated, can long endure. We are met on a great battlefield of that war. We have come to dedicate a portion of that field as a final resting place for those who here gave their lives that that nation might live. It is altogether fitting and proper that we should do this.

But, in a larger sense, we cannot dedicate—we cannot consecrate—we cannot hallow—this ground. The brave men, living and dead, who struggled here have consecrated it, far above our poor power to add or detract. The world will little note, nor long remember, what we say here, but it can never forget what they did here. It is for us the living, rather, to be dedicated here to the unfinished work which they who fought here have thus far so nobly advanced. It is rather for us to be here dedicated to the great task remaining before us—that from these honored dead we take increased devotion to that cause for which they gave the last full measure of devotion—that we here highly resolve that these dead shall not have died in vain—that this nation, under God, shall have a new birth of freedom—and that government of the people, by the people, for the people, shall not perish from the earth.

APPENDIX E

The Second Inaugural Address, Washington, DC

Delivered just six weeks before his assassination, Lincoln's Second Inaugural Address is a dark and ultimately hopeful meditation on the meaning of the Civil War. In the heart of the speech, Lincoln makes the uncanny and prophetic connection between the 250 years of brutal oppression of America's enslaved Black population and the "righteous" scales of justice that have now meted out similar devastation upon America—both North and South—over the course of the war. The healing balm of "malice toward none" (tolerance) and "charity for all" (love) is the redeeming path suggested by Lincoln, in what many consider to be his greatest address—one Frederick Douglass would describe to Lincoln as a "sacred effort." The "suicide" Lincoln prophesied in 1838 at the Lyceum could not be altogether avoided, but its effect upon future generations perhaps might be.

March 4, 1865

Fellow countrymen: At this second, appearing to take the oath of the presidential office, there is less occasion for an extended address than there was at the first. Then a statement somewhat in detail of a course to be pursued seemed fitting and proper. Now, at the expiration of four years during which public declarations have been constantly called forth on every point and phase of the great contest which still absorbs the attention and engrosses the energies of the nation little that is new could be presented. The progress of our arms, upon which all else chiefly depends, is as well known to the public as to myself, and it is, I trust, reasonably satisfactory and encouraging to all. With high hope for the future, no prediction in regard to it is ventured.

On the occasion, corresponding to this four years ago, all thoughts were anxiously directed to an impending civil war. All dreaded it—all sought to avert it. While the inaugural address was being delivered from this place devoted altogether to saving the Union without war, insurgent agents were in the city seeking to destroy it without war—seeking to dissolve the Union and divide effects by negotiation. Both parties deprecated war, but one of them would make war rather than let the nation survive, and the other would accept war rather than let it perish. And the war came.

One eighth of the whole population were colored slaves not distributed generally over the Union but localized in the Southern part of it. These slaves constituted a peculiar and powerful interest. All knew that this interest was somehow the cause of the war. To strengthen, perpetuate, and extend this interest was the object for which the insurgents would rend the Union, even by war, while the government claimed no right to do more than to restrict the territorial enlargement of it. Neither party expected for the war, the magnitude. or the duration which it has already attained. Neither anticipated that the cause of the conflict might cease with, or, even before the conflict, itself should cease. Each looked for an easier triumph and a result less fundamental and astounding. Both read the same Bible and pray to the same God, and each invokes His aid against the other. It may seem strange that any men should dare to ask a just God's assistance in wringing their bread from the sweat of other men's faces, but let us judge not that we be not judged. The prayers of both could not be answered—that of neither has been answered fully. The Almighty has His own purposes. "Woe unto the world because of offenses for it must needs be that offenses come but woe to that man by whom the offense cometh." If we shall suppose that American slavery is one of those offenses which, in the providence of God, must needs come but which having continued through His appointed time He now wills to remove, and that He gives to both North and South this terrible war as the woe due to those by whom the offense came shall we discern therein any departure from those divine attributes which the believers in a living God always ascribe to Him. Fondly do we hope—fervently do we pray—that this mighty scourge of war may speedily pass away. Yet if God wills that it continue until all the wealth piled by the bondsman's two hundred and fifty years of unrequited toil shall be sunk, and until every drop of blood drawn with the lash shall be paid by another drawn with the sword, as was said three thousand years ago, so still it must be said, "The judgments of the Lord are true and righteous altogether."

With malice toward none with charity for all with firmness in the right as God gives us to see the right let us strive on to finish the work we are in to bind up the nation's wounds, to care for him who shall have borne the battle, and for his widow and his orphan—to do all which may achieve and cherish a just and lasting peace among ourselves and with all nations.

ACKNOWLEDGMENTS

Fortunately, scholarship on this period of Lincoln's life has its share of outstanding work. At the head of the list of those to whom I owe a debt of gratitude are historians Kate Masur, Angela D. Ray, and Manisha Sinha, who, in their own work and as contributors to the Lincoln Presidential Foundation's docu-series on the Lyceum Address, sparked fresh insights for me in writing this book. I'm eternally thankful to Erin Carlson Mast, the president of the LPF, for convening us, and for her encouragement along the way. Those from whom I gained tremendous insights into Lincoln and his early political years include Michael Burlingame, Eric Foner, Harold Holzer, Fred Kaplan, David S. Reynolds, Joshua Shenk, Ronald C. White, and Douglas L. Wilson, among many others. The list of Lincoln scholars is dotted with preeminent historians and terrific scholarship. It has been a real joy to visit and, on occasion, revisit the works of those who have devoted far more time in their careers to Lincoln than I have. They remain standard-bearers in the field—and a personal inspiration. I'd also like to single out Walter Johnson's work as particularly insightful about lynching and mob violence, subjects we are painfully obliged to return to again and again.

I'd also like to thank Rutgers University Librarian Natalie Borisovets, Harvard Law School Research Services Librarian Jennifer Allison, Library of Congress Reference Assistant

Allison Buser, and Vicksburg's former Old Courthouse Museum Director and Curator George "Bubba" Bolm and his able successor, Jordan Rushing, for their help guiding me along the archival grain. Special thanks go to Chaim Lipskar at Writers House, who went above and beyond in supporting both me and this project in its earliest days. It was Chaim who connected me with my agent Dan Conaway, who has done yeoman's work in helping this book have its day in the sun. On that score, I'm equally grateful to Keith Wallman and the entire team at Diversion Books for helping me share this story of Lincoln with the widest audience possible.

Never far removed from me as I write are my suddenly, unimaginably old triplets—eighteen years old and college-bound. Gabby, Luke, and Daniel, you are the joys of my life, and I can't tell you enough how proud of you I am. You inspire me in your own generational struggle for justice and fairness, and I love you.

NOTES

INTRODUCTION

1. See the C-SPAN rankings for example, where Jackson falls nine places over the past twenty years; Wilson falls seven. James K. Polk—closely associated with Jackson historically—likewise is the only other president in the top twenty to lose ground, dropping five places. https://www.c-span.org/presidentsurvey2021/?page=overall.
2. Sean Wilentz, *The Rise of American Democracy: Jefferson to Lincoln* (W. W. Norton & Co.: New York, 2005), 455.
3. Alexis de Tocqueville, *Democracy in America* (Chicago: University of Chicago Press, 2000), 12.
4. "These objects [concerning race] which touch on [democracy], do not enter into it; they are American without being democratic," he wrote. Alexis de Tocqueville, *Democracy in America*, 303.
5. Sheldon Wolin, *Tocqueville Between Two Worlds* (Princeton: Princeton University Press, 2001), 74.
6. See Federalist 55, https://avalon.law.yale.edu/18th_century/fed55.asp.
7. Ted Robert Gurr, *Violence in America: Protest, Rebellion, Reform* (London: Sage Publications, 1989), 42.
8. Paul Frymer, *Building an American Empire: The Era of Territorial and Political Expansion* (Princeton: Princeton University Press, 2017), 4, 7.
9. David Walker Howe, *What Hath God Wrought: The Transformation of America, 1815–1848* (Oxford: Oxford University Press, 2007), 432.
10. David Walker Howe, *What Hath God Wrought*, 423–30.

11. See Douglas L. Wilson on Herndon, for example. Douglas L. Wilson, *Honor's Voice: The Transformation of Abraham Lincoln* (New York: Vintage Books, 1998), 12.
12. William H. Herndon and Jesse W. Weik. (Douglas L. Wilson and Rodney O. Davis, eds.), *Herndon's Lincoln* (Champaign, IL: University of Illinois Press, 2016), 126.
13. Fred Kaplan, *Lincoln: A Biography of a Writer* (New York: Harper Perennial, 2008), 77–80.
14. Garry Wills, *Lincoln at Gettysburg: The Words That Remade America* (New York: Simon & Schuster, 2006), 154–55.
15. Kenneth S. Greenberg, *Honor & Slavery* (Princeton: Princeton University Press, 1996), 143.
16. William E. Gienapp, *This Fiery Trial*: *The Speeches and Writings of Abraham Lincoln* (Oxford: Oxford University Press, 2002), 9–13. The entire paragraph from this part of the speech is simply gone.
17. See the University of Michigan's site for the Lyceum Address: https://quod.lib.umich.edu/j/jala/2629860.0006.103/—perpetuation-of-our-political-institutions-address?rgn=main;view=fulltext.
18. Henry Louis Gates Jr. (ed. with Donald Yacovone), *Lincoln on Race and Slavery* (Princeton: Princeton University Press, 2009), 3.
19. Walter Johnson, *The Broken Heart of America: St. Louis and the Violent History of the United States* (New York: Basic Books, 2020) and Michael J. Pfeifer, ed., *Lynching Beyond Dixie: American Mob Violence Outside the South* (Urbana: University of Illinois Press, 2013), 73.
20. Elijah P. Lovejoy, *Memoir of of the Rev. Elijah P. Lovejoy* (Rockton, IL: Digital Ninjas Media, 2016), 122.
21. Walter Johnson, *The Broken Heart of America*, 2013.
22. Walter Johnson, *The Broken Heart of America*, 3.
23. For James Short's letter to William Herndon, July 7, 1865, see Douglas L. Wilson and Rodney O. Davis, *Herndon's Informants: Letters, Interviews, and Statements About Abraham Lincoln* (Urbana: University of Illinois Press, 1998), 73.
24. Eric Foner, *The Fiery Trial: Abraham Lincoln and American Slavery* (New York: W. W. Norton & Co., 2010), 120.

25. Eric Foner, *The Fiery Trial*, 28.
26. Eric Foner, *The Fiery Trial*, xx.

CHAPTER ONE

1. See David Grimsted, *American Mobbing, 1828–1861: Toward Civil War* (Oxford: Oxford University Press, 1998), 144–45. See also: Thomas Shackelford, "Proceedings of the Citizens of Madison County, Mississippi, at Livingston, in July 1835, in Relation to the Trial and Punishment of Several Individuals Implicated in a Contemplated Insurrection in This State" (Jackson, Mississippi, 1836). A pamphlet in the Rare Book Room, Library of Congress, Washington, DC.
2. Jeff Forret and Bruce E. Baker, eds., *Southern Scoundrels: Grifters and Graft in the Nineteenth Century* (Baton Rouge: Louisiana State University Press, 2021), 18.
3. Walter Johnson, *River of Dark Dreams: Slavery and Empire in the Cotton Kingdom* (Cambridge, MA: Belknap Press, 2013), 69–70.
4. The 1838 novel was William Gilmore Simms's *Richard Hurdis: A Tale of Alabama* (Forret and Baker), 24.
5. David J. Libby, *Slavery and Frontier Mississippi, 1720–1835* (Jackson, MS: University Press of Mississippi, 2004), 110.
6. For the original account of Turner's confession, see Thomas R. Gray, Nat Turner, and Paul Royster (Depositor), "The Confessions of Nat Turner (1831)," Electronic Texts in American Studies, https://digitalcommons.unl.edu/etas/15. For the broader context of fears of Black rebellion related to Haiti, see Leslie M. Alexander, *Fear of a Black Republic: Haiti and the Birth of Black Internationalism in the United States* (Urbana: University of Illinois, 2023).
7. Recorded in the "Proceedings of the citizens of Madison county, in the State of Mississippi, at Livingston, in July, 1835, in relations to the Trial and Punishment of several individuals, implicated in a contemplated Insurrection of the Slaves in that state, as reported by the Committee of Safety" [noted by the author going forward as "Proceedings at Livingston"] in Virgil A. Stewart's *The History of Virgil A. Stewart and His Adventure in Capturing and Exposing the Great "Western Land Pirate" and His Gang, in Connexion with the Evidence; Also of the Trials, Confessions, and Execution of a Number of*

Murrell's Associates in the State of Mississippi During the Summer of 1835, and the Execution of Five Professional Gamblers by the Citizens of Vicksburg, on the 6th July, 1835 (New York: Harper & Brothers, 1836), 224. The digitized book can be found, courtesy of New York Public Library Collections, at https://archive.org/details/historyofvirgilaoohowa. All italics in citations are original.

8. Douglas L. Wilson, *Honor's Voice: The Transformation of Abraham Lincoln* (New York: Vintage Books, 1998), 90.

9. Abraham Lincoln, "Communication to the People of Sangamon County," March 9, 1832. *Collected Works of Abraham Lincoln. Volume 1.* University of Michigan digitized collection. https://quod.lib.umich.edu/l/lincoln/lincoln1/1:8?rgn=div1;view=fulltext.

10. See David S. Reynolds, *Abe: Abraham Lincoln in His Times* (New York: Penguin Books, 2020), 120–21, and Josiah Gilbert's *The Life of Abraham Lincoln* (Legare Street Press, 2022), 39. Gilbert's Life was originally published by Gurdon Bill in 1866. The one thousand dollars Lincoln owed in 1835 would be roughly thirty-five thousand dollars today.

11. Michael Burlingame, *Abraham Lincoln: A Life* (Baltimore: Johns Hopkins University, 2023), 34. Italics in original.

12. David S. Reynolds, *Abe*, 134.

13. Douglas L. Wilson, *Honor's Voice*, 81.

14. See Joshua Wolf Shenk, *Lincoln's Melancholy: How Depression Challenged a President and Fueled His Greatness* (New York: First Mariner Books, 2005), 82–83.

15. Abraham Lincoln, "Communication to the People of Sangamo County," March 9, 1832.

16. Abraham Lincoln, "Communication to the People of Sangamo County," March 9, 1832.

17. Abraham Lincoln, "Communication to the People of Sangamo County," March 9, 1832.

18. Abraham Lincoln, "Communication to the People of Sangamo County," March 9, 1832.

19. It was James Matheny, a future groomsman in Lincoln's wedding, who recognized Lincoln's handwriting. It was also "J. Matheny" who advertised Lincoln's Lyceum Address in the *Sangamo Journal* in January of 1838. Michael Burlingame, *Abraham Lincoln: A Life*, 95.

20. See William Henry Herndon, *Herndon's Lincoln: The True Story of a Great Life* (Chicago: Belford, Clarke & Company, 1889), 92; and David Herbert Donald, *Lincoln* (New York: Simon & Schuster, 1995), 38–39.
21. David Herbert Donald, *Lincoln*, 39.
22. David Herbert Donald, *Lincoln*, 40.
23. David Herbert Donald, *Lincoln*, 40–41, 55.
24. See H. Donald Winkler, *Lincoln's Ladies: The Women in the Life of the Sixteenth President* (Nashville: Cumberland House, 2004), 42–43.
25. H. Donald Winkler, *Lincoln's Ladies*, 62–63.
26. Douglas L. Wilson, *Honor's Voice*, 109–11.
27. Michael Burlingame, *Abraham Lincoln: A Life*, 97.
28. Michael Burlingame, *Abraham Lincoln: A Life*, 98. Misspellings and punctuation in original.
29. Michael Burlingame, *Abraham Lincoln: A Life*, 98.
30. David S. Reynolds, *Abe*, 48–49.
31. See Douglas L. Wilson, *Honor's Voice*, 127, 183–84.
32. Fred Kaplan, *Lincoln: The Biography of a Writer* (New York: HarperCollins, 2008), 101.
33. For an excellent analysis of the veracity of the relationship between Lincoln and Rutledge, see James M. McPherson's *This Mighty Scourge: Perspectives on the Civil War* (Oxford: Oxford University Press, 2007), 190–93.
34. James M. McPherson, *This Mighty Scourge*, 117.
35. James M. McPherson, *This Mighty Scourge*, 117.
36. Michael Burlingame, *Abraham Lincoln: A Life*, 99.
37. David Herbert Donald, *Lincoln*, 56.
38. Michael Burlingame, *Abraham Lincoln: A Life*, 99.
39. Catherine Clinton, *Mrs. Lincoln: A Life* (New York: HarperCollins, 2009), 40.
40. Douglas L. Wilson, *Honor's Voice*, 117.
41. H. Donald Winkler, *Lincoln's Ladies*, 81.
42. H. Donald Winkler, *Lincoln's Ladies*, 81.
43. Michael Burlingame, *Abraham Lincoln: A Life*, 99–100.

44. Michael Burlingame, *Abraham Lincoln: A Life*, 100.
45. Michael Burlingame, *Abraham Lincoln: A Life*, 100.
46. Don E. Fehrenbacher and Virginia Fehrenbacher, eds. *Recollected Words of Abraham Lincoln* (Stanford: Stanford University Press, 1996), 184.
47. "The Suicide's Soliloquy," *Sangamo Journal*, August 25, 1838. For why the poem was most likely Lincoln's, see Joshua Wolf Shenk, *Lincoln's Melancholy*, 41. https://idnc.library.illinois.edu/?a=d&d=SJO18380825.2.180.
48. "Mobs at Vicksburg," *Sangamo Journal*, July 25, 1835. Digitized by Illinois Digitized News Collection, *Illinois State Journal*. http://www.idaillinois.org/digital/collection/eiu02/id/7048.
49. "Vicksburgers of 19th Century Stormed Gamblers' Stronghold," *Clarion-Ledger*, March 26, 1950. Article in Historical Society file, Old Courthouse Museum, Vicksburg, Mississippi.
50. Vicksburg Register. "*From the Vicksburg Register*," *The Floridian* (July 25, 1835). (2020, December 07). In *Encyclopedia Virginia*, https://encyclopediavirginia.org/primary-documents/from-the-vicksburg-register-the-floridian-july-25-1835.
51. "Mobs at Vicksburg," *Sangamo Journal*, July 25, 1835.
52. "Insurrection of Slaves in Mississippi," *Sangamo Journal*, August 1, 1835. Digitized by Illinois Digitized News Collection, *Illinois State Journal*.
53. "Insurrection of Slaves in Mississippi," *Sangamo Journal*, August 1, 1835.
54. I'm thankful to Jordan Rushing, curator of the Old Courthouse Museum in Vicksburg, Mississippi, for sharing the museum's documents related to the city's gamblers with me. He also walked me through the March 22, 1848, map of the city, directing my gaze to the old kangaroo district. For the etymological and cultural origins of kangaroo courts, see Barry Popik, "Kangaroo Court," *The Big Apple*, August 4, 2006, cited in *Historical Dictionary of American Slang*, 1997.2:336. I'm immensely grateful for the Museum's fellow curator George "Bubba" Bolm's assistance as well. Author's in-person visit, November 30, 2023.
55. For a rich and detailed account of Stewart's conspiracy and the "Murrell Excitement," see Sandlin's account in *Wicked River*. Lee Sandlin, *Wicked River, The Mississippi When It Last Ran Wild* (Vintage, 2010), 142–70.
56. Cincinnati's Public Library provides a digitized copy of the pamphlet. See https://digital.cincinnatilibrary.org/digital/collection/p16998coll17/id/29194.

57. Lee Sandlin, *Wicked River*, 148.
58. Mark Twain, *Mark Twain: Mississippi Writings* (Washington, DC: Library of Congress, 1982), 405.
59. *Mark Twain: Mississippi Writings*, 69–70.
60. Cited from "The Vicksburg Outrage," *Vicksburg Whig*, August 13, 1835. https://www.newspapers.com/image/225025163.
61. Virgil A. Stewart, *The History of Virgil A. Stewart*, 268. https://archive.org/details/historyofvirgilaoohowa/page/268/mode/2up?view=theater&q=gamblers.
62. Manfred Berg, *Popular Justice: A History of Lynching in America* (Lanham, MD: Ivan R. Dee, Publisher, 2011), 37. Italics in original.
63. Ben Wynne, *The Man Who Punched Jefferson Davis: The Political Life of Henry S. Foote, Southern Unionist* (Baton Rouge: Louisiana State University Press, 2018), 25–26.
64. Douglas L. Wilson and Rodney O. Davis, eds., *Herndon's Informants: Letters, Interviews, and Statements About Abraham Lincoln* (Urbana: University of Illinois Press, 1997) , 23
65. Letter from R. N. Rutledge, October 21, 1866, in William Henry Herndon, *Herndon's Lincoln*, 139.
66. See Joshua Wolf Shenk, *Lincoln's Melancholy* for a compelling discussion, 19–21.
67. Herman Melville, *Billy Budd, Bartleby, and Other Stories* (New York: Penguin Books, 2016), 300.
68. Mentor Graham letter, April 2, 1866. Douglas L. Wilson and Rodney O. Davis, eds., *Herndon's Informants*, 143.
69. David S. Reynolds, *Abe*, 157.
70. Michael Burlingame, *Abraham Lincoln: A Life*, 100.
71. Michael Burlingame, *Abraham Lincoln: A Life*, 100.
72. Douglas L. Wilson and Rodney O. Davis, eds., *Herndon's Informants*, 440.
73. Michael Burlingame, *Abraham Lincoln: A Life*, 101.
74. Michael Burlingame, *Abraham Lincoln: A Life*, 101–102.
75. Herndon letter to Jesse Weik, January 1891. William H. Herndon, *Herndon on Lincoln: Letters* (Urbana: University of Illinois Press, 2016), 334.

76. William H. Herndon, *Herndon on Lincoln: Letters*, 334.

CHAPTER TWO

1. Paul Simon, *Freedom's Champion: Elijah Lovejoy* (Carbondale, IL: Southern Illinois University Press 1994), 45.
2. "Steamboat Travel on the Mississippi," *New York Times*, April 18, 1864.
3. Paul Simon, *Freedom's Champion*, 45.
4. US Astronomical Applications Department. https://aa.usno.navy.mil/calculated/rstt/year?ID=AA&year=1836&task=0&lat=38.63&lon=-90.25&label=St.+Louis%2C+MO&tz=6&tz_sign=-1&submit=Get+Data.
5. Louis S. Gerteis. *Civil War St. Louis* (Lawrence: University Press of Kansas, 2001), 6.
6. Louis S. Gerteis. *Civil War St. Louis.*
7. US Census data. https://www2.census.gov/library/working-papers/1998/demographics/pop-twps0027/tab07.txt.
8. Walter Johnson, *The Broken Heart of America: St. Louis and the Violent History of the United States* (New York: Basic Books, 2020), 74.
9. Walter Johnson, *The Broken Heart of America*, 73–76. See also: "Horrible Tragedy," *Sangamo Journal* (from the *St. Louis Republic*), May 7, 1836. Center for Research Libraries, Digitized Collection. https://dds.crl.edu/crldelivery/19083.
10. "Horrible Tragedy," *Sangamo Journal* (from the *St. Louis Republic*), May 7, 1836.
11. Paul Simon's account, for example, says McIntosh was told he'd have to serve five years. See Paul Simon, *Freedom's Champion*, 45. David S. Reynolds writes that McIntosh's violent reaction to his arrest was the result of a "policeman [having] threatened his friends."
12. Paul Simon, *Freedom's Champion*, 46.
13. "Horrible Tragedy," *Sangamo Journal* (from the *St. Louis Republic*), May 7, 1836. Center for Research Libraries, Digitized Collection. https://dds.crl.edu/crldelivery/19083.
14. Walter Johnson, *The Broken Heart of America*, 74.
15. John F. Darby, *Personal Recollections of John F. Darby* (St. Louis: Hawthorn Publishing, 1880), 152.

16. John F. Darby, *Personal Recollections of John F. Darby*, 152. The *Sangamo Journal*'s report from the *St. Louis Republic*, numbers the mob at "several thousand persons."
17. "Burning Alive," *The Liberator*, May 21, 1836. http://fair-use.org/the-liberator/1836/05/21/the-liberator-06-21.pdf. Text can also be found in Christopher Waldrep, *Lynching in America: A History in Documents* (New York: New York University Press, 2006), 54–55.
18. Charles Dickens, "Charles Dickens Letter to John Forster," April 14, 1842, in *The Letters of Charles Dickens: The Pilgrim Edition, Vol. 3: 1842–1843* (Oxford University Press, 1974), 197.
19. John F. Darby, *Personal Recollections of John F. Darby*, 152.
20. Elijah P. Lovejoy, *Memoir of the Rev. Elijah P. Lovejoy* (Rockton, IL: Digital Ninjas Media, 2016), 122.
21. Walter Johnson, *The Broken Heart of America*; and Michael J. Pfeifer, ed., *Lynching Beyond Dixie: American Mob Violence Outside the South* (Urbana: University of Illinois Press, 2013), 73.
22. Sidney Blumenthal, *A Self-Made Man: The Political Life of Abraham Lincoln, 1809–1849* (New York: Simon & Schuster, 2016), 167.
23. Thomas M. Spencer (ed.), *The Other Missouri History: Populists, Prostitutes, and Regular Folk, Vol. I* (Columbia, MO: University of Missouri Press, 2004), 73.
24. Alexis de Tocqueville, *Democracy in America* (Harvey C. Mansfield and Delba Winthrop [eds.], Chicago: University of Chicago Press, 2000), 343.
25. Thomas M. Spencer (ed.), *The Other Missouri History*, 73.
26. Louis S. Gerteis. *Civil War St. Louis*, 13.
27. David S. Reynolds, *John Brown, Abolitionist: The Man Who Killed Slavery, Sparked the Civil War, and Seeded Civil Rights* (New York: Vintage Books, 2005), 64–65.
28. Mark J. Miller, *Cast Down: Abjection in America, 1700–1850* (Philadelphia: University of Pennsylvania Press, 2016), 109.
29. "The Lynching of Francis McIntosh," Reparative Justice Coalition of St. Louis, 2021, https://www.rjcstl.org/francis-mcintosh-remembrance.

30. "Remembrance of 1836 Lynching of Francis McIntosh," WashU Arts & Sciences, April 30, 2022, https://artsci.washu.edu/events/remembrance-1836-lynching-francis-mcintosh.
31. Michael Burlingame, *Abraham Lincoln: A Life*, 42. James McPherson, among many others, agrees. See James M. McPherson, *Abraham Lincoln* (Oxford: Oxford University Press, 2009), 3.
32. Herman Melville, *Moby-Dick* (New York: Penguin Classics, 2002), 6.
33. Eric Foner, *Free Soil, Free Labor, Free Men: The Ideology of the Republican Party Before the Civil War* (Oxford: Oxford University Press, 1995), xvii.
34. See David S. Reynolds, *Abe*, 88–89.
35. David S. Reynolds, *Abe*, 88.
36. Michael Burlingame, *Abraham Lincoln: A Life*, 44.
37. Henry Louis Gates Jr. (ed.), *Lincoln on Race & Slavery* (Princeton: Princeton University Press 2009), 9.
38. Abraham Lincoln to Mary Speed, September 27, 1841. *Abraham Lincoln to Mary Speed.* [1841-09-27]. /documents/D200280. The Papers of Abraham Lincoln Digital Library.
39. Abraham Lincoln to the editor of the *Sangamo Journal*. [1836/06/23]. /documents/D200076. The Papers of Abraham Lincoln Digital Library.
40. Abraham Lincoln to the editor of the *Sangamo Journal*.
41. Abraham Lincoln to the editor of the *Sangamo Journal*.
42. See Donald on the 1836 campaign. David Herbert Donald, *Lincoln*, 59–60.
43. William Henry Herndon, *Herndon's Lincoln*, 115–116.
44. William E. Gienapp, *Abraham Lincoln and Civil War America: A Biography* (Oxford: Oxford University Press, 2002), 22.
45. David S. Reynolds, *Abe*, 188.
46. As quoted by William Herndon. See Michael Burlingame, *Abraham Lincoln: A Life*, 91.
47. Joshua Wolf Shenk, *Lincoln's Melancholy*, 4.
48. Joshua Wolf Shenk, *Lincoln's Melancholy*, 22. Periods added by author.
49. Douglas L. Wilson, *Honor's Voice*, 193.
50. Douglas L. Wilson and Rodney O. Davis, eds., *Herndon's Informants*, "L. M. Greene, letter to William Herndon, May 3, 1866," 250.

51. William Henry Herndon, *Herndon's Lincoln*, 136.
52. Joshua Wolf Shenk, *Lincoln's Melancholy*, 149.
53. Joshua Wolf Shenk, *Lincoln's Melancholy*, 149.
54. See Douglas L. Wilson, *Honor's Voice*, 135.
55. Letter, Abraham Lincoln to Mary S. Owens, August 16, 1837. Library of Congress. Manuscript/Mixed Material. http://www.loc.gov/item/mcc.030/.
56. Joshua Wolf Shenk, *Lincoln's Melancholy*, 22.
57. Michael Burlingame, ed., *An Oral History of Abraham Lincoln: John G. Nicolay's Interviews and Essays* (Carbondale, IL: Southern Illinois University Press, 1996), 22.
58. "Young Men's Lyceum Will Meet on Saturday Evening, the 12, Inst." *Sangamo Journal*, November 12, 1836. Center for Research Libraries, Digitized Collection, p. 2, column 7. https://dds.crl.edu/crldelivery/19083.

CHAPTER THREE

1. Ronald C. White Jr., *A. Lincoln: A Biography* (New York: Random House, 2009), 335.
2. Abraham Lincoln, *Autobiography of Abraham Lincoln* (Zinc Read, 2023), 16.
3. "Collected Works of Abraham Lincoln. Volume 1 [1824-Aug. 28, 1848]." In the digital collection *Collected Works of Abraham Lincoln*. https://name.umdl.umich.edu/lincoln1. University of Michigan Library Digital Collections. Accessed August 27, 2024.
4. Michael Burlingame, *Abraham Lincoln: A Life*, 122.
5. Michael Burlingame, *Abraham Lincoln: A Life*, 122.
6. "Collected Works of Abraham Lincoln. Volume 1 [1824-Aug. 28, 1848]." In the digital collection *Collected Works of Abraham Lincoln*. https://name.umdl.umich.edu/lincoln1. University of Michigan Library Digital Collections. Accessed August 27, 2024.
7. Ronald C. White Jr., *A. Lincoln: A Biography*, 75.
8. Ronald C. White Jr., *A. Lincoln: A Biography*, 122.
9. See Office of the Illinois Secretary of State. https://www.ilsos.gov/departments/archives/online_exhibits/100_documents/1853-black-law.html.

10. See William E. Gienapp, ed., *This Fiery Trial: The Speeches and Writings of Abraham Lincoln* (Oxford: Oxford University Press, 2002), 8; Eric Foner, *The Fiery Trial: Abraham Lincoln and American Slavery* (New York: W.W. Norton & Co., 2010), 26; David S. Reynolds, *Abe*, 143; and Ronald C. White Jr., *A. Lincoln: A Biography*, 76.
11. Douglas L. Wilson, *Honor's Voice*, 165.
12. Abraham Lincoln to Albert G. Hodges, April 4, 1864. Gienapp, 194.
13. *Sangamo Journal*, August 6, 1836, page 2, column 1. Digitized by Illinois Digitized News Collection, *Illinois State Journal*. https://idnc.library.illinois.edu/?a=d&d=SJO18360813.2.9.
14. Paul Simon, *Freedom's Champion: Elijah Lovejoy* (Carbondale: Southern Illinois University Press, 1994), 1–3.
15. Paul Simon, *Freedom's Champion: Elijah Lovejoy*, 6
16. For a detailed account of Lovejoy's journey, see Ken Ellingwood, *First to Fall: Elijah Lovejoy and the Fight for a Free Press in the Age of Slavery* (New York: Pegasus Books, 2021), 20–22.
17. Ken Ellingwood, *First to Fall*, 8–9.
18. Ken Ellingwood, *First to Fall*, 25–26.
19. Ken Ellingwood, *First to Fall*, 27.
20. Ken Ellingwood, *First to Fall*, 63–64.
21. Elijah P. Lovejoy to Owen Lovejoy, August 26, 1833. Joseph C. Lovejoy and Owen Lovejoy, *Memoir of the Rev. Elijah P. Lovejoy: Who Was Murdered in Defense of the Liberty of the Press at Alton, Illinois November 7, 1837* (Digital Ninjas Media, 2016), 66.
22. Ken Ellingwood, *First to Fall*, 68.
23. Ken Ellingwood, *First to Fall*, 75.
24. Ken Ellingwood, *First to Fall*, 118–19.
25. Joseph C. Lovejoy and Owen Lovejoy, *Memoir of the Rev. Elijah P. Lovejoy*, 119.
26. Joseph C. Lovejoy and Owen Lovejoy, *Memoir of the Rev. Elijah P. Lovejoy*, 11.
27. Ken Ellingwood, *First to Fall*, 80.
28. Ken Ellingwood, *First to Fall*, 81.

29. Joseph C. Lovejoy and Owen Lovejoy, *Memoir of the Rev. Elijah P. Lovejoy*, 156. Emphasis in original.
30. Paul Simon, *Freedom's Champion: Elijah Lovejoy*, 43.
31. Paul Simon, *Freedom's Champion: Elijah Lovejoy*, 48
32. Joseph C. Lovejoy and Owen Lovejoy, *Memoir of the Rev. Elijah P. Lovejoy*, 172.
33. Ken Ellingwood, *First to Fall*, 103–04.
34. Joseph C. Lovejoy and Owen Lovejoy, *Memoir of the Rev. Elijah P. Lovejoy*, 176.
35. Ken Ellingwood, *First to Fall*, 109.
36. Collected Works of Abraham Lincoln. Volume 1. Lincoln, Abraham, 1809-1865. https://quod.lib.umich.edu/l/lincoln/lincoln1/1:101?rgn=div1;view=fulltext.
37. Ken Ellingwood, *First to Fall*, 126.
38. Richard B. Kielbowicz, "The Law and Mob Law in Attacks on Antislavery Newspapers, 1833–1860." *Law and History Review* 24, no. 3 (2006): 559–600. http://www.jstor.org/stable/27641403.
39. Seventh debate, Abraham Lincoln and Stephen Douglas, October 15, 1858, Alton, Illinois. https://www.nps.gov/liho/learn/historyculture/debate7.htm.
40. Robert S. Harper, *Lincoln and the Press* (New York: McGraw Hill Book Company, Inc), 1951, 2–3.
41. Merton Lynn Dillon. "The Antislavery Movement in Illinois: 1824–1835." *Journal of the Illinois State Historical Society (1908–1984)* 47, no. 2 (1954): 152. http://www.jstor.org/stable/40189370.
42. July 4th Address by William M. Stewart, *Sangamo Journal*, August 6, 1836, page 1, column 3. Digitized by Illinois Digitized News Collection, *Illinois State Journal*. https://libsysdigi.library.uiuc.edu/OCA/Books2010-01/illinoisnewspape118651934illi/illinoisnewspape118651934illi_djvu.txt.
43. Joshua F. Speed, *Reminiscences of Abraham Lincoln and Notes of a Visit to California* (Louisville: John F. Morton and Company, 1884), 21.
44. David S. Reynolds, *Abe*, 136–37.
45. Michael Burlingame, *Abraham Lincoln: A Life*, 138.

46. Michael Burlingame, *Abraham Lincoln: A Life*, 138. See also, David S. Reynolds, *Abe*, 137—"tore the hide off Ewing."
47. David S. Reynolds, *Abe*, 137.
48. David S. Reynolds, *Abe*, 138.
49. Michael Burlingame, *Abraham Lincoln: A Life*, 115.
50. David Herbert Donald, *Lincoln*, 63.
51. David Herbert Donald, *Lincoln*, 63.
52. David Herbert Donald, *Lincoln*, 64.
53. Ronald C. White Jr., *A. Lincoln: A Biography*, 79; David Herbert Donald, *Lincoln*, 66.
54. David Herbert Donald, *Lincoln*, 66.
55. David S. Reynolds, *Abe*, 141–42.
56. Lincoln letter to Mary Owens, May 7, 1837. Roy P. Basler, ed., *Collected Works of Abraham Lincoln* (New Brunswick: Rutgers University Press, 1953-55), 178-79.
57. William H. Herndon and Jesse William Weik, *Herndon's Lincoln: A True Story of a Great Life* (Cosimo, Incorporated, 2009), 160–61. "Deeply wounded," in Donald, 69.
58. David Herbert Donald, *Lincoln*, 68.
59. Joseph C. Lovejoy and Owen Lovejoy, *Memoir of the Rev. Elijah P. Lovejoy*, 254–55.
60. Englewood, 219.
61. Thomas Jefferson, *Notes on the State of Virginia*. See Query 14. https://docsouth.unc.edu/southlit/jefferson/jefferson.html.
62. Collected Works of Abraham Lincoln. Volume 3. Lincoln, Abraham, 1809-1865. https://quod.lib.umich.edu/l/lincoln/lincoln3/1:20.1?rgn=div2;view=fulltext.
63. Englewood, 220–25.
64. Joseph C. Lovejoy and Owen Lovejoy, *Memoir of the Rev. Elijah P. Lovejoy*, 88–91.
65. Englewood, 268.
66. For a vivid and richly detailed account of Lovejoy's final hours, see Englewood, 269–81.

67. See Sidney Blumenthal, *A Self-Made Man: The Political Life of Abraham Lincoln, Volume I, 1809–1849* (New York: Simon & Schuster, 2017), 165.
68. See Englewood, 284–85.
69. "On the Perpetuation of Our Political Institutions," *Sangamo Journal*, February 3, 1838.
70. Englewood, 289.
71. "Voice of the Press: the Alton Murder," *The Liberator*, December 8, 1837. https://www.digitalcommonwealth.org/book_viewer/commonwealth:8k71q215z.
72. Englewood, 292.
73. David S. Reynolds, *John Brown, Abolitionist*, 64–65.
74. Janet Kemper Beck, *Creating the John Brown Legend: Emerson, Thoreau, Douglass, Child and Higginson in Defense of the Raid on Harpers Ferry* (Jefferson, NC: McFarland and Company, 2009), 32.
75. Janet Kemper Beck, *Creating the John Brown Legend*, 32.
76. Abraham Lincoln Temperance Address, February 22, 1842. *Collected Works of Abraham Lincoln*. Volume 1. Lincoln, Abraham, 1809–1865. https://quod.lib.umich.edu/l/lincoln/lincoln1/1:294?rgn=div1;view=fulltext.
77. William F. Moore and Owen Lovejoy, *Collaborators for Emancipation: Abraham Lincoln and Owen Lovejoy* (Urbana: University of Illinois Press, 2014), 1.
78. William F. Moore and Owen Lovejoy, *Collaborators for Emancipation*, 103.
79. Melvin Jameson, *Elijah Parish Lovejoy as a Christian* (Rochester: Scranton, Wetmore, & Co., 1838), 113. https://upload.wikimedia.org/wikipedia/commons/a/ad/Elijah_Parish_Lovejoy_as_a_Christian_%28IA_elijahparishlove00jameiala%29.pdf.
80. Abraham Lincoln to James Lemen, March 2, 1837. "Letter from Abraham Lincoln to James Lemen," House Divided: The Civil War Research Engine at Dickinson College, https://hd.housedivided.dickinson.edu/node/109. See also Carl Sandburg, who includes the letter in his biography of Lincoln. Carl Sandburg, *Abraham Lincoln: The Prairie Years, Volumes One and Two* (Rahway: Harcourt, Brace and Company, 1926), 170–71. Finally, David S. Reynolds cites from the letter in his *John Brown, The Man Who Killed Slavery, Sparked the Civil War, and Seeded Civil Rights* (New York: Vintage Press, 2006), 62.

CHAPTER FOUR

1. William Henry Herndon, *Herndon's Lincoln: A True Story of a Great Life* (New York: Cosimo, Inc, 2009), 126.
2. "Aspect of the Times," *Sangamo Journal*, August 29, 1835, page 3, column 4. Digitized by Illinois Digitized News Collection, *Illinois State Journal*. https://idnc.library.illinois.edu/?a=d&d=SJO18350829.2.12.
3. *Sangamo Journal*, May 3, 1838. Center for Research Libraries, Digitized Collection. https://dds.crl.edu/crldelivery/19083.
4. *Sangamo Journal*, May 3, 1838.
5. See Garry Wills, *Lincoln at Gettysburg: The Speech that Made America* (New York: Simon & Schuster, 2006), 42–44.
6. *Sangamo Journal*, May 3, 1838.
7. Peoria speech, October 16, 1854. https://www.nps.gov/liho/learn/historyculture/peoriaspeech.htm.
8. *Sangamo Journal*, January 26, 1839. https://idnc.library.illinois.edu/?a=d&d=SJO18390126.
9. *Sangamo Journal*, February 2, 1839. https://idnc.library.illinois.edu/?a=d&d=SJO18390202.
10. Angela G. Ray, "Learning Leadership: Lincoln at the Lyceum, 1838." *Rhetoric and Public Affairs* 13, no. 3 (2010): 349–87. http://www.jstor.org/stable/41936458.
11. *Sangamo Journal*, May 3, 1838. Center for Research Libraries, Digitized Collection. https://dds.crl.edu/crldelivery/19083.
12. Thomas F. Schwartz, "The Springfield Lyceums and Lincoln's 1838 Speech." *Illinois Historical Journal* 83, no. 1 (1990): 45–49. http://www.jstor.org/stable/40192388.
13. See Angela G. Ray, *The Lyceum and Public Culture in the Nineteenth-Century United States* (East Lansing: Michigan State University Press, 2005).
14. Angela G. Ray, "Learning Leadership: Lincoln at the Lyceum, 1838."
15. Angela G. Ray, *The Lyceum and Public Culture in the Nineteenth-Century United States*, 21.
16. See Harold Holzer, *Lincoln at Cooper Union: The Speech that Made Abraham Lincoln President* (New York: Simon & Schuster, 2006).

17. Thomas F. Schwartz, (1990). "The Springfield Lyceums and Lincoln's 1838 Speech." *Illinois Historical Journal, 83*(1), 45–49. http://www.jstor.org/stable/40192388.
18. July 4th Address by William M. Stewart, *Sangamo Journal*, August 6, 1836, page 1, column 3. Digitized by Illinois Digitized News Collection, *Illinois State Journal*. https://idnc.library.illinois.edu/?a=d&d=SJO18360806.2.5.
19. July 4th Address by William M. Stewart, *Sangamo Journal*, August 6, 1836.
20. July 4th Address by William M. Stewart, *Sangamo Journal*, August 6, 1836.
21. July 4th Address by William M. Stewart, *Sangamo Journal*, August 6, 1836.
22. July 4th Address by William M. Stewart, *Sangamo Journal*, August 6, 1836.
23. "On the Perpetuation of Our Political Institutions," Springfield, Illinois, January 27, 1838. https://quod.lib.umich.edu/j/jala/2629860.0006.103/—perpetuation-of-our-political-institutions-address.
24. Abraham Lincoln, Gettysburg Address, November 19, 1863, https://www.loc.gov/item/rbpe.24404500/.
25. Abraham Lincoln, Gettysburg Address, November 19, 1863.
26. "On the Perpetuation of Our Political Institutions," Springfield, Illinois, January 27, 1838.
27. Abraham Lincoln (1865), *Second inaugural address of the late President Lincoln*. James Miller, New York. [Pdf] Retrieved from the Library of Congress, https://www.loc.gov/item/2020770559/.
28. "On the Perpetuation of Our Political Institutions," Springfield, Illinois, January 27, 1838. Italics added for emphasis.
29. See David S. Reynolds, *Abe*, 58.
30. Herman Melville, *Moby-Dick*, 559.
31. For Starbuck's contemplation, see Herman Melville, *Moby-Dick*, 559. The story of Naboth and Ahab can be found in 1 Kings 21:1–14 (King James Version). "And Ahab spake unto Naboth, saying, Give me thy vineyard, that I may have it for a garden of herbs, because it is near unto my house: and I will give thee for it a better vineyard than it; or, if it seem good to thee, I will give thee the worth of it in money, And Naboth said unto Ahab, The LORD forbid it me, that I should give the inheritance of my fathers unto thee."
32. Thurston Clarke, *Ask Not: The Inauguration of John F. Kennedy and the Speech that Changed America* (New York: Penguin Books, 2010), 75.

33. "On the Perpetuation of Our Political Institutions," Springfield, Illinois, January 27, 1838. Italics added for emphasis.
34. Edward Gibbons, *History of the Decline and Fall of the Roman Empire* (New York: Penguin Books, 2001).
35. For contemporary interest in Franklin's quote, see: "'A republic if you can keep it': Did Ben Franklin really say Impeachment Day's favorite quote?" *Washington Post*, December 18, 2019. https://www.washingtonpost.com/history/2019/12/18/republic-if-you-can-keep-it-did-ben-franklin-really-say-impeachment-days-favorite-quote/.
36. Jack Rakove, *A Politician Thinking: The Creative Mind of James Madison* (Norman, OK: University of Oklahoma Press, 2017), 55.
37. See Daniel Farber's *Lincoln's Constitution* (Chicago: University of Chicago Press, 2004).
38. For the *Federalist Papers*, see the Library of Congress's online collection. https://guides.loc.gov/federalist-papers/full-text.
39. "On the Perpetuation of Our Political Institutions," Springfield, Illinois, January 27, 1838.
40. Alexis de Tocqueville, *Democracy in America*, 275.
41. "On the Perpetuation of Our Political Institutions," Springfield, Illinois, January 27, 1838.
42. "On the Perpetuation of Our Political Institutions," Springfield, Illinois, January 27, 1838.
43. "On the Perpetuation of Our Political Institutions," Springfield, Illinois, January 27, 1838.
44. See Harvey C. Mansfield's interview with Bill Kristol for an interesting exchange on this idea translated into English from Tocqueville's *Democracy in America*. https://www.youtube.com/watch?v=SJ9dIYd-vUQ.
45. Federalist 1. https://guides.loc.gov/federalist-papers/full-text.
46. "On the Perpetuation of Our Political Institutions," Springfield, Illinois, January 27, 1838.
47. "On the Perpetuation of Our Political Institutions," Springfield, Illinois, January 27, 1838.
48. Abraham Lincoln, December 1, 1862, National Archives. See Miller Center of Public Affairs, University of Virginia online transcription. https://miller-

center.org/the-presidency/presidential-speeches/december-1-1862-second-annual-message.

49. See Lerone Bennett, Jr.'s *Forced Into Glory: Abraham Lincoln's White Dream* (Chicago: Johnson Publishing Company, 2000), for this same criticism of Lincoln's politics.

50. "On the Perpetuation of Our Political Institutions," Springfield, Illinois, January 27, 1838.

51. See Ronald Reagan Presidential Library and Museum for text. January 20, 1981. https://www.reaganlibrary.gov/archives/speech/inaugural-address-1981.

52. George Washington Farewell Address, September 19, 1796. See Constitution Center's online text. https://constitutioncenter.org/the-constitution/historic-document-library/detail/george-washington-farewell-address-1796.

53. "On the Perpetuation of Our Political Institutions," Springfield, Illinois, January 27, 1838.

54. Federalist 10.

55. See Linda Kerber's "The Republican Mother: Women and the Enlightenment-An American Perspective," *American Quarterly* 28, no. 2 (1976): 187–205. https://doi.org/10.2307/2712349.

56. "On the Perpetuation of Our Political Institutions," Springfield, Illinois, January 27, 1838.

57. Major L. Wilson, "Lincoln on the Perpetuation of Republican Institutions: Whig and Republican Strategies," *Journal of the Abraham Lincoln Association* 16, no. 1 (1995): 15–25, http://www.jstor.org/stable/20148916. 22-23.

58. "On the Perpetuation of Our Political Institutions," Springfield, Illinois, January 27, 1838.

59. "On the Perpetuation of Our Political Institutions," Springfield, Illinois, January 27, 1838.

60. Douglass Adair, *Fame and the Founding Fathers* (Carmel, IN: Liberty Fund), 1998.

61. "On the Perpetuation of Our Political Institutions," Springfield, Illinois, January 27, 1838.

62. "On the Perpetuation of Our Political Institutions," Springfield, Illinois, January 27, 1838.

63. Baxter's talk is truly a remarkable example of fine public lecturing—another thing about to disappear. Charles Baxter, "Things About to Disappear," August 20, 2017. https://sites.middlebury.edu/blwc/bread-loaf-writers-conference/2017-audio-recordings/.

64. "On the Perpetuation of Our Political Institutions," Springfield, Illinois, January 27, 1838.

65. Matthew 16:18 (KJV)

66. Matthew 16:18 (KJV).

67. William Henry Herndon, *Herndon's Lincoln*, 126.

68. Abraham Lincoln, June 16, 1858, "House Divided Speech," Springfield, Illinois. Lincoln, Abraham, excerpt from "Famous speeches [of] Digital Public Library of America, https://dp.la/item/1ca86fc8c80f378ffd703603369523aa.

69. These outstanding and highly influential works are Ronald C. White Jr.'s *Lincoln's Greatest Speech: The Second Inaugural Address* (New York: Simon & Schuster, 2006), Harold Holzer's *Lincoln at Cooper Union: The Speech that Made Abraham Lincoln President* (New York: Simon & Schuster, 2005), and Garry Wills's *Lincoln at Gettysburg: The Words that Remade America* (New York: Simon & Schuster, 2006).

CHAPTER FIVE

1. Farewell Address, February 11, 1865. https://www.nps.gov/liho/learn/historyculture/farewell.htm.

2. "Mr. Lincoln Again at Home," *New York Times*, May 4, 1865.

3. In the end, this oft-quoted line delivered to the editor Horace Greeley proved to be a great political feint, as Lincoln would announce his plans for emancipation thirty days later. "Abraham Lincoln Papers: Series 2. General Correspondence. 1858 to 1864: Abraham Lincoln to Horace Greeley, Friday Clipping from August 23, 1862," *Daily National Intelligencer*, Washington, DC, 1862. Manuscript/Mixed Material. https://www.loc.gov/item/mal4233400/.

4. "Lincoln on Roosevelt," *New York Times*, October 3, 1912. The reader incorrectly dates the Lyceum to January 27 of 1837, instead of 1838.

5. Nathaniel Philbrick, *Why Read Moby-Dick?* (New York: Penguin Books, 2013), 6.

6. Senator Joseph McCarthy, February 9, 1950. Copied the text: Joseph McCarthy. "Address to the League of Women Voters, Wheeling, West Virginia," Speech, February 09, 1950. From Teaching American History, https://teachingamericanhistory.org/document/address-to-the-league-of-women-voters-wheeling-west-virginia-2/ (accessed May 6, 2023).
7. "Fact check: False quote attributed to Abraham Lincoln is distortion of an 1838 speech," *Reuters*, January 26, 2021. https://www.reuters.com/article/uk-factcheck-lincoln-quote-fake/fact-check-false-quote-attributed-to-abraham-lincoln-is-distortion-of-an-1838-speech-idUSKBN29V2HH.
8. James Silverman, "The Hedgehog and the Fox: Lincoln's Lyceum Address for the Ages," September 22, 2021. https://www.friendsofthelincolncollection.org/lincoln-lore/6804/.
9. Brian F. Danoff, "Lincoln, Machiavelli, and American Political Thought," *Presidential Studies Quarterly* 30, no. 2 (2000): 290–311, http://www.jstor.org/stable/27552095.
10. John Channing Briggs, *Lincoln's Speeches Reconsidered* (Baltimore: Johns Hopkins University Press, 2005), 2.
11. "Mr. Lincoln and the Enduring Danger," *New York Times*, February 16, 1958.
12. Harry V. Jaffa, *Crisis of the House Divided: An Interpretation of the Lincoln-Douglas Debates* (Chicago: University of Chicago Press), 183.
13. Harry V. Jaffa, *Crisis of the House Divided*, 191.
14. Harry V. Jaffa, *Crisis of the House Divided*, 224.
15. Harry V. Jaffa, *Crisis of the House Divided*, 195.
16. Michael Burlingame, *Abraham Lincoln: A Life*, 142.
17. Google. "Ngram Viewer: 'lyceum speech.'" Google Books Ngram Viewer. https://books.google.com/ngrams/graph?content=lyceum+speech&year_start=1800&year_end=2019&corpus=en-2019&smoothing=3.
18. See for example, David Grimsted's *American Mobbing, 1828-1861* (Oxford: Oxford University Press, 1998).
19. David Herbert Donald, *Lincoln*, 588.
20. "Documenting Reconstruction Violence," Equal Justice Initiative. https://eji.org/report/reconstruction-in-america/documenting-reconstruction-violence/#chapter-3-intro
21. See James Allen's *Without Sanctuary: Lynching Photography in America* (Santa Fe, NM: Twin Palms Publishers, 1999).

22. "These Are the People Who Died in Connection With the Capitol Riot," *New York Times*, October 13, 2022.
23. "On the Perpetuation of Our Political Institutions," Springfield, Illinois, January 27, 1838.
24. "How George Floyd Was Killed in Police Custody," *New York Times*, May 31, 2020.
25. "The Charlottesville Rally five years later," NPR, August 12, 2022. https://www.npr.org/2022/08/12/1116942725/the-charlottesville-rally-5-years-later-its-what-youre-still-trying-to-forget.
26. Liz Cheney, "Our Constitutional Moment: The Danger to the Rule of Law," American Enterprise Institute, September 22, 2022, https://www.aei.org/research-products/report/our-constitutional-moment-the-danger-to-the-rule-of-law/.
27. Liz Cheney, "Our Constitutional Moment."
28. Jamie Raskin, "This Cannot Be the Future of America," Democracy Now, February 10, 2021. Transcript, https://www.democracynow.org/2021/2/10/jamie_raskin_impeachment_trial_capitol_insurrection.
29. "House narrowly approves $1.9B to fortify Capitol after riot," *Associated Press*, May 20, 2021. https://apnews.com/article/donald-trump-capitol-siege-riots-government-and-politics-5a2319f8bc63521a6314faa55c55ae33.
30. "Students Walk Out After Being Told to Limit Black History Program." Yahoo News, February 7, 2023. Accessed July 8, 2025. https://www.yahoo.com/lifestyle/alabama-students-stage-walkout-allegedly-174005862.html.
31. Eric Foner, *The Fiery Trail*, xx.

APPENDIX

Source: *Collected Works of Abraham Lincoln*, edited by Roy P. Basler et al.

ABOUT THE AUTHOR

CREDIT: Photo courtesy of the author

SALADIN AMBAR is a professor of political Science and a senior scholar at the Center on the American Governor at Rutgers University's Eagleton Institute of Politics. He is the winner of the Association of American Publishers' PROSE Best Book Award in Government and Politics for *Stars and Shadows: The Politics of Interracial Friendship from Jefferson to Obama*, and his *Malcolm X at Oxford Union: Racial Politics in a Global Era* is in development for a feature film. He is codirector of the Democracy Committee for New Jersey's Reparations Council and was a contributor for the Lincoln Presidential Foundation's docuseries on the Lyceum Address. Ambar hosts the podcast *This Moment in Democracy* and has been a fact-checker and contributor for the Smithsonian Channel, CNN's *Race for the White House*, and PBS's *MetroFocus*. He is the father of teenaged triplets and lives in Philadelphia.